THE BAFFLED PARENT'S GUIDE TO
COACHING YOUTH
BASKETBALL

09

THE BAFFLED PARENT'S
GUIDE TO
Coaching Youth
BASKETBALL

David Faucher

Head Coach, Dartmouth College Men's Team

With Nomad Communications
Norwich, Vermont

Ragged Mountain Press/McGraw-Hill

Camden, Maine • New York • San Francisco • Washington, D.C. • Auckland
Bogotá • Caracas • Lisbon • London • Madrid • Mexico City • Milan • Montreal
New Delhi • San Juan • Singapore • Sydney • Tokyo • Toronto

To my three sons—Mike, Joe, and Scott

Ragged Mountain Press

A Division of The **McGraw-Hill** Companies

10 9 8 7 6 5 4 3

Library of Congress Cataloging-in-Publication Data
Faucher, David.
    The baffled parent's guide to coaching youth basketball / David Faucher.
      p.   cm.
    Includes index.
    ISBN 0-07-134607-4
    1. Basketball for children—Coaching. 2. Basketball for children—Training.
    I. Title.
    GV886.25.F38   1999   99-29248
    796.323'07'7—dc21   CIP

Questions regarding the content of this book should be addressed to
Ragged Mountain Press
P.O. Box 220
Camden, ME 04843
www.raggedmountainpress.com

Questions regarding the ordering of this book should be addressed to
The McGraw-Hill Companies
Customer Service Department
P.O. Box 547
Blacklick, OH 43004
Retail customers: 1-800-262-4729
Bookstores: 1-800-722-4726

This book is printed on 70-lb. Citation
Printed by Quebecor Printing, Fairfield, PA
Design by Carol Gillette
Production by Eugenie Delaney and Dan Kirchoff
Edited by Tom McCarthy, Alex Barnett, and Jane M. Curran
Unless otherwise specified, photography by Mark Austin-Washburn

Contents

Part One

Coaching 101: The Coach's Little Instruction Manual

Part Two

Drills: The Foundation for Growth, Happiness, and a Coach's Peace of Mind

Introduction: So You Said You'd Be the Coach, Huh?

So, you're a Baffled Parent.

You thought you were going to drop your daughter off at the rec department for a meeting on the upcoming basketball season and maybe stand in the background until the teams were picked. But before you could hide, you found yourself "appointed" coach of one of the teams, though "captured" might be more appropriate. Now you're in for it. You've never coached anything, let alone something that looks as chaotic as basketball. You never even *played* basketball, for that matter.

Don't worry, help is at hand.

This book is designed to help any coach have a successful season—and by successful I don't mean more wins than losses. The advice and drills here are aimed at helping you teach 6- to 12-year-old boys and girls the basics of basketball, sportsmanship, teamwork, and, above all else, the fun and rewards of the game.

No book purporting to offer such advice will work unless it recognizes the differences, sometimes quite marked, in your players' abilities and responses to your coaching style—though everyone reacts positively to encouragement and praise. I'll show you how to deal with this mix, easily. Some kids are natural athletes, some aren't. Some kids may come to the first practice knowing more about the game than you. Others won't have a clue. Some will be anxious to learn, while others will be nervous about playing. Some won't be able to sit still or stop talking; others will sit quietly in the background. Girls, especially as they become older, might respond quite differently to criticism and instruction. I recognize this and give you advice on dealing with such issues throughout the book.

How to Use This Book

Coaching Youth Basketball: The Baffled Parent's Guide is a grab bag of drills, skills, tricks, and techniques. While you should certainly read the book as a whole, it is best digested in smaller bits. The book is designed so novice and experienced coaches alike can teach their players—and perhaps themselves—the basics of good basketball, including fundamental skills and offensive and defensive plays. You'll find advice on every facet of coaching. Part 1, Coaching 101: The Coach's Little Instruction Manual, will give you all the information you need to get started. Need to brush up on the very basics of basketball? Start with chapter 2, Before Hitting the Court: Basketball in a Nutshell, and chapter 4, Essential Skills—and How to Teach Them. These chapters will tell you most everything you need to know before your first practice, including basic rules and the reasons the skills and drills are important and how the drills will help your team become stronger and better basketball players. And speaking of the first practice, are you truly baffled about how to get organized? Chapter 1, Creating an Atmosphere of Good Habits, and chapter 3, Setting Up the Season, will clear things up.

In part 2, Drills: The Foundation for Growth, Happiness, and a Coach's Peace of Mind, you'll find specific step-by-step drills to help you with fundamentals and with offensive and defensive skills—all designed to grow with you during the season. Drills are numbered consecutively by type (for example, **F2** is Fundamental drill 2, Power Jumps), and for your quick reference I've labeled them

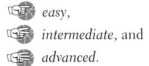

easy,

intermediate, and

advanced.

These designations will help you determine which drills to use. Any drill designated *easy* is appropriate for a beginning player: there are no prerequisites. An *intermediate* drill assumes that a player has mastered elementary skills and has learned some basic basketball terminology. A drill labeled *advanced*—and there are few in this book—assumes the player has game experience and is familiar enough with the game to understand the context of the drill.

At the end of many chapters you'll find a helpful question-and-answer section dealing with hard-to-handle situations that could arise during the season, and throughout the book there are useful sidebars to ease your anxieties. You'll also find a detailed index to locate advice on specific problems, a glossary of basketball terms, a list of resources, and diagrams of referee signals.

Remember, one size does not fit all. You'll have to be able to adapt to the many, sometimes conflicting, demands placed on you. The tools to help are right here.

A Word on Coaching Style

While the drills and techniques I've provided here have all worked for me for years, they fit *my* coaching style. A lot of my drills and games are set up as minicompetitions with winners and losers. Basketball is a competitive sport, and that's why most of the kids are playing it. I like to give little forfeits to the losers, like sprinting the floor, doing a few push-ups, or whatever. These forfeits are always easy and meant to be fun little penalties. They are never meant to be punishments or negative in any way. I've found that they encourage the competitive aspect of practice and are great motivators. If you feel the kids you are coaching are too young, or you just don't like "consequences," it's completely up to you. Choose what feels comfortable and leave the rest.

One good coach might be very vocal, another calm and quiet. There's no one right coaching style, but there are wrong ones. If you can keep your temper, never disparage the players or the referees, seek constantly to teach and encourage, and finish the season with improved players who enjoy the game and each other—then I don't need to see your won-loss record to know you're a good coach.

Remember that your goal is to make this basketball experience fun for your players. This is a time when kids should learn to work as a team while having a great time. As their coach, you are an important role model with an opportunity to teach this group of children many life lessons, in addition to sport-specific skills: to respect each other as individuals; to work together as a team; to view competition, both winning and losing, as part of the overall experience rather than an end in itself; and, above all, to have fun while discovering the skills of a game they can enjoy for a lifetime. These are all lessons you can help them learn, and you'll be surprised at what you can learn in the process.

Whatever your coaching credentials, your greatest responsibility is to give each team member a positive learning experience while teaching them some skills and helping them be the best individuals and teammates they can be. You can do it.

There are five keys to being a good coach:

Remember the Scouting motto: always be prepared. Every time you walk out onto the court, have a plan for what you want to accomplish during practice that day. Know what drills and plays you'll work on and how long you want to spend on each one. Make sure that you are familiar enough with what you plan to do so that you can present it clearly. By organizing your thoughts and preparing a practice plan ahead of time, you'll keep the kids moving, interested, and learning.

On the other hand, be flexible: if it isn't working, do something else. You don't have to be a psychiatrist to judge when kids are motivated and having fun, and when they are bored. You can have a great practice plan on paper, but if for some reason it's not going well, be ready to change your plan and move on to something else.

Good words go a long way: keep it positive. Everyone loves praise and encouragement. Make sure that one of your cardinal rules is that the coach is the only person *ever* to criticize a player—and then only in a positive, constructive way. Kids should never criticize other kids. And remember that kids never can hear enough of "Great job," "Nice try," and "Good work." Positive encouragement is vital to a positive experience.

Keep your energy level high. You need to match the energy level of the kids you'll be coaching and to show excitement and enthusiasm about the game, every time, all the time. Psych yourself up before each practice so that you are excited and energized from the moment you step onto the court. Your players will feed off of your energy, and everyone will have a better practice because of it.

Keep your eyes open and get to know your team. One of the best ways to learn to coach your team effectively is to observe. Watch your players carefully; get to know their personalities. You'll learn a lot by just watching how they react and interact with each other. And be sure to learn every player's name right away—they need the recognition and will respond positively to it.

Photo by Jeff Karufman/FPG International

PART ONE

Coaching 101:
The Coach's Little
Instruction Manual

CHAPTER 1

Creating an Atmosphere of Good Habits

The Essentials

You need to have discipline as a coach for the same reason you need to have discipline as a parent: things don't get done unless there is a leader who knows when and how to take charge and be in control. A big part of coaching is learning how to organize and control group behavior and to create an atmosphere of good habits through positive energy and reinforcement. The key to teaching kids to respond to your signals and direction is to do it through fun, not dictatorial, activities. You'll be dealing with different personalities and skill levels—some who are eager to please, others who don't listen as well, possibly one or two who are sullen or stubborn, still others who aren't as physically adept—but you can treat everybody the same in encouraging the positive and reinforcing good team behavior. In this way you'll create an atmosphere that's fun and supportive, an atmosphere where the kids feel special by doing what is expected of them.

Good habits are just that: actions that need to be consistently reinforced and practiced. It's important to establish a routine of behavior for every practice, not only because kids need and crave routine, but also because it reinforces your role as the person in charge. Every day, whether your kids are age 7 or 12, start practice the same way: you blow the whistle, and the kids come to you. That's how practice should start every day of the season, with no variations. When they are gathered around you, explain what will take place during practice: outline the drills they will perform, the skills they will learn, and what you expect to get out of the practice. Then send them off to do the drills or skills or whatever with a team cheer.

At the end of every practice, whistle the team in again. Quickly summarize what you accomplished in practice and reinforce the positive things that took place. If someone did something well, acknowledge it. If the players didn't do something well, mention what you want to work on the next time. Keep it positive, and keep them motivated. End every practice with a

Whistle in the team for a meeting at the beginning of every practice to outline what will happen during the session. Hold a second meeting at the end of every practice to highlight what was accomplished and point out areas that need work.

reminder of when and where the next practice or game is, and disband the players with another team cheer. Never vary from holding the meeting at both the beginning and end of practice, no matter how tired you are or how late you are running. The kids need the feedback and reinforcement that they are doing a good job.

Establish Your Identity as Coach

Your players need to know what to call you—you're going to have your own children, your friends' children, and kids you don't know on your team. Whatever you decide you want to be called—"Coach," another nickname, or your first or last name—make sure to keep it consistent. For however long practice lasts, everyone—your kids, your neighbors' kids, and kids who don't know your name—calls you the same thing, everyone plays by the same rules, and everyone is treated with the same respect and encouragement.

Let Your Signal Be Their Guide

At the beginning of the very first day of practice, stand in the center of the court, blow your whistle and signal the kids in. Most of the players will probably shoot one or two last baskets, run around for a minute more, and then make their way over to you. Gather them around and explain that when you blow the whistle, they are to come to you without shooting any more baskets or bouncing any balls. Encourage them to move to you quickly and enthusiastically, as a team. Send them back out onto the court with enthusiastic encouragement. Blow the whistle again. If they don't respond the way you've explained, do it again until every player on the team comes immediately to the circle when the whistle is blown. When the team gets it right, reinforce that enthusiastically—tell them that they're working like a team—and have them acknowledge it, too, by giving themselves three claps on your signal.

Drills That Promote Teamwork, Concentration, and Good Habits

The following drills should be a consistent part of your practices. Not only do they reinforce your role as the authority figure and team leader, but they also inspire great teamwork.

Drill 1: Listening

How: Instruct your team to do an activity on your signal. For example, tell them to clap their hands whenever you cross yours. Give them a number to call out every time you hold up your hand. Work on their listening skills, using plenty of enthusiasm and encouragement, until every player gets it right.

Why: The point of these drills is to have your players focused on you and what you are saying, as well as instilling in them a sense of team accomplishment from the outset.

Simple games resembling Simon Says, in which players perform some action upon a cue, promote listening skills, attention to the coach, and team cohesion.

Drill 2: Teamwork

How: Gather your players together. Tell them they have 30 seconds from the time you say, "Go!" to line up on the center line from shortest to tallest. Blow your whistle at the end of 30 seconds and have the players freeze. If they don't accomplish the task, give them positive encouragement, make them do five push-ups, and then give them the drill again. They'll get it eventually, and they'll learn to work together as a team to do it.

Why: The point here is to get your players to work together right away. This drill also acknowledges and positively reinforces the differences between players so that all are valuable to the team.

Drill 3: Foot Fire

How: Spread your team members out so they have room to move. Have them bend at the knees and flex at the waist. On the whistle, have them move from foot to foot as rapidly as they can. When you blow the whistle, they make a half turn with a quick jump. Do this several times, changing direction, making a full turn, crossing feet, etc. If their interest or energy is flagging, move on to something else.

Why: This drill combines following directions from the coach with improving agility in a fun way. It is exceptionally flexible and can be used for virtually any sport.

Players of all levels will benefit from the Foot Fire drill, which develops agility and paying attention to the coach.

Drill 4: Peer Pressure Shooting

How: First a note on this drill. As I said in the introduction, I think the minicompetitions encourage the competitive aspect of the game. If you have trouble with doling out "consequences," that's fine. It's a matter of style. For this drill, pick one player to come to the foul line. Tell your team that if their peer makes the shot, they'll all get a reward (a piece of candy, no sprints that day—choose something that you know they'll really like and that you are prepared to supply). If the player doesn't make the shot, the whole team has to run up and down the court. Let the player take the foul shot. If the shot is made, have every team member congratulate the shooter. If the shot isn't made, judge the reaction of the players. If you see frowns or comments, bring the kids together. Explain the situation that has just taken place: here's a kid out on the foul line with the burden of the whole team on his or her shoulders. Ask them, "Who misses on purpose?" And then ask them to think about how the shooter is feeling, rather than how they are feeling. Instruct them that before they pay the forfeit and line up again, they should give the shooter a high five and some positive encouragement that reflects how that player—not the others—must be feeling.

Why: This drill helps players understand what it feels like to be the person on the line, under pressure, and helps them develop an unselfish attitude about success and failure. As you encourage positive reactions to good and bad situations, players learn to be graceful and accepting of others.

Drill 5: Team Huddle and Listening

How: When you're in the huddle explaining what will happen during practice that day, interject the phrase, "We are . . . ," to which your team should respond, "Together!" Do this at unexpected times during the huddle.

Why: This activity keeps kids paying attention to what you are saying, and it also promotes the positive aspect of togetherness that you are trying to instill in your players. The drill helps neutralize ability levels and reinforces that everyone is as important as everyone else. If your players hear and use the term "together" enough, they believe it.

Questions and Answers

Q. It's really clear that one player on my team is only here because his parents want him to participate. He often talks when I'm explaining drills, and then he doesn't know what to do out on the court. How do I get him to become more a part of the team without singling him out for discipline all the time?

A. When you're dealing with young kids, you need to try and do drills that generate activity. This keeps them moving and positive so that they are too busy to have behavior problems. But when one person is taking the attention away from the others, it needs to be addressed. Try the four-strikes-and-you're-out rule. I believe in really working on positive encouragement. For example, if a player is talking while you're explaining something, don't single him out. Instead, remind all the team members that they need to be quiet when the coach is speaking. If you get this player to respond, really reinforce that positive team behavior. If he still doesn't respond, single him out. If the behavior still persists, give him the choice to participate or not—but make it his choice, not yours: "Do you want to play today, or do you want to sit out?" Finally, if nothing else works, make him sit out. But don't leave him there. Get back to him as soon as possible and cultivate him. Suggest he join the group again, and also tell him the behavior shouldn't happen again. If he's okay with that, great. The incident is over. If he's sulking or clearly not okay with that, you should tell him that you and he need to meet with his parents to figure out a solution. The key is to address the problem immediately and to remember that it's okay to demand respect in a positive and consistent way.

Q. I have a player who is consistently very late to practice. It's disruptive because I have to stop whatever I'm doing and explain everything all over again. I know it isn't really her fault because her parents drive her there, but how do I address it?

A. Part of the privilege of playing on a team is respecting the other players on it and the rules the coach has established. As coach, you need to enforce all the rules consistently and fairly. At the beginning of the sea-

Notes from the Floor: About Winning and Losing

One year when I was a high school basketball coach, my team wasn't exceptionally talented, but they all worked very hard. To make it to the state tournament they had to win the last two games. The pressure was on for the second-to-last game, but we didn't win. It was a quiet bus ride back to the gym, and we still had one game left. The next day before practice I was in my office thinking, "Well, we have one more practice, and one last game, and I'm going to really have to go out there and motivate them." Then I walked into the gym, and I felt the spirit of the kids—they were already out there, working hard on their drills, with incredible enthusiasm. They all knew there was no chance for the state tournament, but it didn't affect the way they practiced that day. I was so impressed with my team, and it showed me that winning is really insignificant when you look at the big picture. They had the ability to play the game, it was fun for them, they had made great friends, and watching them bounce back was one of the best experiences I have had as a coach. We played that last game with a lot of pride and intensity against an excellent team on the road—and we won. I went into the locker room after that last game and told my players how proud I was of them, and then I told them to shower up while I went to talk to the parents outside the locker room. Twenty minutes later there was a group of guys still sitting there with their uniforms on. When I asked them what was going on, they said, "Coach, we don't want to take our uniforms off." So they went home all sticky and dirty in their uniforms, just wanting to hold onto the experience a little longer. They showed me that for them, it was the overall experience that was so important, not just winning individual games.

son, explain both in person and in a note sent home to the parents your policies regarding lateness and no-shows without an excuse and asking players to please call if they will be late or unable to attend. Explain in that note what the penalties will be if players don't arrive on time, such as sitting out until you invite them to join practice (which will make lateness somewhat less disruptive) or sitting on the bench during the following game. And stick with the penalties. Don't back down and give "this one kid" an exception unless the situation really calls for it. Call parents directly to try and find a solution to repeated lateness, like carpooling. Certainly you should be flexible if it is an emergency or unforeseen problem, but keep in mind that what's fair for one person on the team is fair for everyone. Be consistent, and the majority of the team and their parents will thank you for it.

Q. I started out the season doing the whistle drill, and for a while it worked great. After a few weeks, though, I had to blow my whistle and then yell, and now I'm yelling and whistling and feel like I've lost control. What should I do?

A. Go back to the basics. The kids are going to want to participate, and you can't let the inmates run the asylum. Kids need and crave routine, and when their routine breaks down, it is reflected in their behavior. Blow the whistle. Wait until everybody is quiet. Remind them of the basics of the whistle drill and have them do it again until

Players should never be allowed to criticize one another. If you do criticize a player, make your remarks positive and encouraging and keep the emphasis on how the team as a whole can improve.

they get it right. Then reinforce their positive response to the whistle. Don't vary from your routine. Use the whistle to bring your team to you. Believe in your leadership.

Q. A few of my players are much better than some of the others, and they have begun criticizing the less-skilled kids. I don't like it, but I can understand the frustration of those kids with better skills. How do I address this?

A. One of my golden rules is that players *never* criticize each other. The only person who is to make any kind of criticism of anyone else is the coach, and you should do it in a tactful, positive, and encouraging way. Gather the team together and discuss the problem, explaining that part of the responsibility of being on a team is to treat everyone with the same amount of respect. Restate the rule about no player-to-player criticism, and explain why you feel that way. Reinforce the idea that everyone has something different and important to offer, and end the meeting with a team cheer. Keep these reminders about being supportive light and upbeat, and the kids will respond.

Before Hitting the Court: Basketball in a Nutshell

Basketball is a fast-moving game that requires strategy and a solid skills foundation to be played successfully, although it can be adapted for all levels of play. It's a great game for all ages, and even young children love the idea of getting the ball through the hoop. This chapter covers the fundamentals of basketball, from rules and essential skills to offensive and defensive basics.

Even if you start out knowing nothing about the game, this chapter will help you get your bearings.

The Court

The game of basketball is played within the boundaries of a basketball court, which is divided in half by the midcourt, or half-court, line (see diagram at right). In boys' basketball the offensive team has 10 seconds to advance the ball past the midcourt line and into its offensive zone; in girls' basketball the team has no time limit. Once the ball is over the midcourt line, it may not be passed or dribbled back over that line by the offensive team. The rectangular area near each basket between the end line (or baseline) and the foul line that is painted and marked by lines (known as the *lane, key,* or *paint*) is the 3-second area. A player on the offense may not be in this area for 3 seconds without receiving the ball. If the player is in this restricted area for 2 seconds and then receives the ball, this player has less than 3 seconds to shoot.

baseline, or end line

corner

block

corner

lane or key

elbow

wing

sideline

foul line extended

three-point arc

foul line

top of circle

midcourt or half-court line

Court terminology. See also the diagram key on page 100.

The Bare Bones

You'll find much of what you need to know about playing and coaching basketball throughout this book. But here's a quick primer for the uninitiated.

- There are five players per side, with substitutions permitted.

- The game is timed and is usually divided into four periods, each lasting 6 to 8 minutes. Each team is permitted a limited number of "time-outs."

- Youth league players are permitted to use smaller balls.

- Each team is assigned a basket, or goal, to defend and tries to shoot the ball through the other basket to score points.

- Teams switch goals after halftime.

- The ball must be advanced by *dribbling*—that is, by bouncing it with either hand. A player who stops a dribble cannot start again and must either pass or shoot. Players may dribble in place or hold the ball without dribbling it for up to 5 seconds without passing or moving the ball if a defender is within 6 feet. Otherwise, there is no time limit.

- Defensive players may block shots, steal passes, or break up dribbles, but both offensive and defensive players must abide by set rules. Violating these rules results in a foul. Depending on the foul, a team might gain possession of the ball or be awarded a free shot at the basket.

- Points are scored by shooting the ball through the hoop. A regular basket, a *field goal*, is worth two points (some leagues permit longer, three-point shots). A *free throw*, a shot awarded to a fouled player, is worth one point.

Basic Rules
Personal Fouls

A *personal foul* is any type of illegal contact, including slapping, holding, pushing, or hitting. Personal fouls are most often committed on an offensive player by a defender, although an offensive player can foul a defender as well. When a foul is charged against an offensive player, the ball is turned over to the opposing team. If an offensive player is fouled while shooting, she is awarded either one, two, or three free throws. If the ball goes in the hoop as the offensive player is fouled, she is awarded the basket and shoots one free throw. If the ball doesn't go in the hoop, she receives two free throws, unless her attempt was behind the three-point arc, which is the area

Other Fouls

Some of the methods you can use to avoid fouls are to teach the defensive players to move their feet and to use only their hands when the ball is clearly exposed to them. Teach them not to reach around the opponent's body to try to steal the ball. When screening, the screener should jump-stop and hold that position. Once a screener sets a screen, she may not lean into the defender—she must be stationary. Players cannot jump into or over another player to try to get a rebound, nor can a player push off or gain any advantage by using her hands on an opponent.

19 feet, 9 inches away from the basket. If a player shoots from behind the arc, she is awarded 3 points.

If an offensive player is not in the act of shooting when fouled, and if the defensive team has not yet reached a total of 7 team fouls in one half, then the ball is given to the offensive team on either the sideline or end line, depending on where on the court the foul occurred. If the defensive team has 7 or more fouls when a foul is committed on an offensive player, then the offensive player receives a "one and one" free throw. This means that if the player makes the first shot, he gets to take another shot; if he misses the first shot, the ball is live, and the game continues. If the defensive team has 10 or more fouls in one half, then the offensive player takes two free throws.

Other personal fouls include these three: *reaching in*, a defender reaches in to steal the ball and makes contact with the dribbler; *over the back*, a player jumps over the back of the opposition on a rebound; *illegal pick*, a player tries to set a pick but either moves his feet or throws an elbow, making contact with the opposition.

Charging

This *offensive foul* (a foul committed by the team with the ball) consists of illegal personal contact by pushing or moving into an opponent's torso, most likely when an offensive player drives to the basket and "runs over" a defensive player.

Blocking Foul

A *blocking foul* is illegal personal contact that impedes the progress of an opponent, most likely when a defensive player "bodies" an offensive player who is driving to the hoop.

Flagrant Foul

A *flagrant foul* involves violent contact with an opponent, including punching, kneeing, or kicking.

Intentional Foul

An *intentional foul* occurs when the player is not directly going for or playing the ball.

When a contested ball cannot be decided without undue roughness a *held ball* is called.

Technical Foul

A *technical foul* is a violation committed by either a player or a coach. It involves no contact with an opponent or contact while the ball is dead. Examples include vulgarity, profanity, or obscene gestures.

Held Ball

A *held ball* occurs when two or more players from opposing teams are in possession of the ball, and control cannot be obtained without undue roughness. At the professional, college, and high school levels, possession is decided with a jump ball, equivalent to a hockey face-off. In youth leagues, however, possession commonly goes to the team on defense. If it is unclear which team is on defense, possession is decided by the possession arrow at the scorer's table. In some leagues, possession following a held ball alternates from one team to the other.

3-Second Rule

An offensive player must move out of the lane, key, or paint (the rectangular area designated on the court between the foul line and the end line) before 3 seconds elapse (see diagram on page 13). In the event of a violation, the ball is awarded to the team on defense. There is no 3-second restriction for defensive players.

Carrying or Palming

Carrying, or *palming*, is a violation that occurs when an offensive player dribbles the ball so that it rests and stays in the palm of the hand.

Double Dribble

Once a player stops dribbling, he cannot start again. A *double dribble* is called when an offensive player stops dribbling, grasps the ball with both hands, and then continues to dribble. It may also be called if the offensive player dribbles with both hands touching the ball simultaneously.

Traveling

If an offensive player "runs" with the ball or moves her pivot foot after she's stopped dribbling, she has *traveled*. When a player holds the ball without dribbling, she can move only one foot, "pivoting" around the foot that can't leave the floor. (Think of the pivot foot as nailed to the ground; it can be turned but not lifted.) The limits to pivoting are as follows:

1. An offensive player can use a two-foot stop after catching a pass or dribbling, where both feet touch simultaneously. In this case the first foot moved is legal, and the other foot becomes the pivot foot.

2. If an offensive player uses a one-two stop, with the feet landing one after the other, the first foot that touches the ground becomes the pivot foot, and the other foot can be lifted or moved legally.

The pivot foot can be lifted (but not returned to the floor before the ball is released) if the offensive player is attempting a shot or a pass, but not a dribble. Pivoting is described in greater detail later in this chapter.

Backcourt Violations

Once the offense brings the ball over the midcourt line, the offense cannot go back across the line. If the ball or even a portion of the foot of the ball handler does cross the line, the other team gets possession. If the offense is making an inbounds pass on the side, they can pass it back over the line, however.

Substitutions

You can substitute players on any dead ball situation—at a whistle, a time-out, or the start of a new quarter or half. Make sure your player first goes to the scorer's table and reports to the scorer. You may substitute for any and all players, except for the shooter in a free throw situation. You can substitute before free throws and between free throws.

Inbounding

There are a number of occasions when a ball must be put into play from either the sideline or end line: after a basket, after a foul shot, when the ball is knocked out-of-bounds, or at the start of the second half. A player has 5 seconds with any inbound pass to get the ball into play.

If a player from Team A last touches the ball before it goes out of bounds, Team B gains possession and the chance to put the ball into play. If the ball goes out at the sideline, it is put into play at the sideline. If the ball goes out at the end line, the ball is put into play at the end line.

If Team A scores a basket, a player from Team B takes the ball out at the end line and is allowed to run along the end line to find an open player to receive the pass. There is no designated spot from which he or she must pass. This is allowed only if a basket or foul shot has been made.

Time-Outs

There are normally three to five time-outs allowed per half, with the exact number depending on the league. Only the team in possession of the ball during a live ball situation may call a time-out. Either team may call for a time-out during a dead ball. A dead ball occurs when an official blows the whistle and stops the clock. The time-out rule has recently changed, and coaches may now call for a time-out from the sidelines. (Formerly, an active player had to call a time-out from the floor.) Any player may also call a time-out.

Getting Started

The game officially begins with a *jump ball*. A designated player from each team, usually the tallest or the one who jumps the highest, lines up against the other player, with one foot in the center and facing the basket at which her team will shoot. The remaining four players from each team are around the "line," which is the circle in the middle of the court, or spread out. The referee tosses up the ball, and the two jumpers try to tip it to their respective teammates.

Setting Up the Season

You'll be wearing many hats as coach, and one of them will be team administrator. The best way to get your season running smoothly, enabling you to focus your energy on coaching, is to be well prepared for the season ahead.

A Checklist for the Season
Create the Practice and Game Schedule and Send a Letter to Parents

Before you meet any of your players, before a ball is bounced or a shot is taken, you should have a schedule of every game you'll play and every practice you'll conduct for the entire year. Generally, two practices and one game per week is a good working number, both in terms of reserving gym time and in a family's time commitment. Coming to practice less than twice a week can make it difficult for the kids to learn and remember the skills they are working on, and more than this creates a time-commitment problem for many families of primary and middle school students. Have this schedule ready to hand out at the first practice so that every parent has a copy and knows what kind of commitment they are making to the team.

Of course, if your youth league is typical, schedule changes and eleventh-hour conflicts for gym time will be the rule rather than the exception. You'll need a telephone tree to deal with that (see a more detailed explanation of the Phone Tree on page 22).

Include with the schedule a letter addressed to the parents that outlines your philosophy and the expectations you have for sportsmanship and participation during the season (see the sample letter later on page 23). Parents—and players—will need to both hear and see what you expect from them in terms of competition, good sportsmanship, being on time, and so on. This provides everyone with a good reference and helps keep everyone clear on why their kids are participating on your team.

Call the Parents before the Season

Once you have the names of the players who are on your team, you should call their parents personally to introduce yourself. Tell them when the first practice is and explain that you'll go over your plans for the whole season at that time. It's a nice personal beginning for parents to get a call from the coach in advance. This also gives you a chance to explain to each parent your expectations for the season, your philosophy about winning and losing, and what you hope your players will learn from the experience. It gives the parents an opportunity to express privately their views and concerns about the season and the expectations they have for their children.

Solicit Parent Help

That first phone call is an ideal time to assess parental enthusiasm for volunteering, carpooling, working out the phone tree, and other administrative help. By all means take advantage of parents who want to help you in some way, especially with administrative duties, and if you can get commitments from parents right away for specific tasks, great. The fewer off-court details you need to take care of, the better.

Meet with Everyone the First Practice

Have parents come to practice on the first day so that you can meet them face-to-face and reiterate what you expect from your team members, their parents, and yourself during the season. The meeting should be short and to the point, but it will reinforce your role as the head of the team and will refresh everyone's memory about why the players are there—and what you expect from them, including being on time and behaving appropriately during practices and games. It is good for the parents to hear your expectations regarding this, since the parents will have a major impact on your players' timeliness to practice and attitudes to discipline and authority.

The first meeting is also an important opportunity to solicit volunteer help during practices. Throw out the idea that anybody is welcome to help you during practice. Stress that you will organize each practice and will have a plan for what to do, so that anytime someone wants to step on the floor and assist you, you will have a defined job for him or her. As volunteer coaches, they will take direction from you, the head coach. There will be many opportunities for using these volunteers.

You can divide the team into two groups, and your volunteer coach can take one group to one end of the court and have the kids do five foul shots each, while you work on another drill with the other group. You can do a dribbling drill, and the parent coach can put varying numbers of fingers up to help the kids practice dribbling with their heads up. Or a parent volunteer might referee a three-on-three game (with three rather than five

Appropriate Numbers for Youth Teams

The ideal number for a youth basketball team is 10 players (remember there are 5 positions on the court). More than 10 can be really unfair for everyone involved. If a team has 16 players, for example, they should be divided into two teams of 8. All 16 may practice together (you'll want an assistant), but the two teams should have a separate schedule of games. It will be more difficult for the players to learn, have fun, and get excited about the great sport of basketball if a coach is trying to juggle 16 kids in a 24-minute game, because the kids just won't get enough playing time.

players a side). While your volunteer helps with drills, you can monitor the group, or the volunteer can step in and work with a player who doesn't have a partner. These are the basic ways to use a volunteer. Even if you don't have a direct assignment, the assistant can encourage and help with the fundamentals. You will be pleasantly surprised at how many parents enjoy taking part and how much help it can be for you.

Equipment

The equipment needs for basketball are simple. Players need a pair of shorts, a pair of sneakers (preferably basketball-friendly), and a ball. Basketball-friendly sneakers are footwear made for basketball or tennis. The sole of the shoe is flat and made of a hard rubber. This will help prevent sprained ankles and will not make marks on a wooden floor. A typical running shoe is not proper footwear for hoops. I would also encourage a high-top sneaker extending above the ankle for greater support.

You may find that your recreation department supplies you with only two to three balls for a team of 10 to 15 players. This is a real problem, since it makes learning the game difficult and much less fun for your players. There should be a ball for every player or every two players on your team. If you don't have enough balls for this, strongly encourage your players to bring a ball from home if they have one. It's important to note that youth-size balls are available. Kids should write their names and phone numbers on their balls to avoid mix-ups. Alternatively, buy several balls, either through a fund-raiser, parental donations, or a personal investment (bought in bulk, balls are quite inexpensive), so that at least every two players on your team will have use of a ball. This is one aspect of your season that you absolutely need to work out beforehand. You don't want to arrive at practice the first day and realize you have three balls for 15 kids.

Water bottles are not essential, but if players bring their own water it can sure reduce the traffic jam at the water fountain. I've found that kids will drink more if they aren't being rushed by the line of teammates behind them. Players should be encouraged to bring their own water and to label those bottles.

Calling All Volunteers!

If you have parents who want to be a part of the team but don't want to help out on the court, by all means use their enthusiasm to take over the administrative end of the season. There are some routine but important administrative aspects of your team's season that could be taken over by a team manager or divided among several committed parents:

- **Phone tree.** You don't want 15 kids calling you—or conversely, to have to call them—every time there's a change in the schedule. Have your manager or a volunteer parent arrange a phone tree, where you call one designated person, who initiates a reliable chain of communication for the rest of the team.

- **Practice transportation.** A designated parent can help arrange carpooling to ensure that every child has a ride to practice and then home afterward. Many families won't need this kind of help, but for others it can make the difference between being able to participate or having to quit because of chronic transportation problems.

- **Away-games transportation schedule.** It's a great idea to have a central meeting place when your team is going to away games. The manager or volunteer parent should set up a schedule of where and when to meet before away games and should provide a sheet of directions for everyone at the meeting place. Meeting in a central place before going to an away game is a good idea for two reasons: it provides a sense of team unity even before the game starts, and it also ensures that everyone is going to the right place at the right time.

- **Equipment and uniforms.** Many youth league players come to their first few practices without the proper equipment. One way to avoid this is to have the manager or another parent arrange a sign-up night at the local sports store so that the kids are signed up for the team and outfitted at the same time. If you're playing in a league that requires a uniform (maybe a T-shirt with a logo or a name on it), remember that most sports stores will give significant discounts to team purchases.

- **Team dinners, fund-raisers, and all that other stuff.** Most youth league teams need to raise money for one thing or another, and any team worth its stuff will have at least one team dinner during the season. The manager or another parent should be in charge of these events and should take advantage of the talents and expertise of the other parents on the team as well.

- **Snack duties.** Kids can be hungry when practice or a game is immediately after school, and a light snack might give them the energy to plunge right into basketball. Or, perhaps you'd like to offer a snack after practice or a game as a fun way for the team to spend a bit of time socializing together. The parent in charge of snacks can either provide the snack each time or can arrange a rotating schedule for other parents to do the job. This is a fun and easy way to get parents involved with the team.

Key to Success: Put That in Writing

Here are some issues that you may want to address in your letter to parents:

- Your coaching philosophy, including attitude toward winning and losing, motivation for playing, teamwork.

- Expectations for sportsmanship and behavior on and off court in practice and games—for players, parents, and you.

- Goals for the season: what you want the players to get out of it, what you want to get out of it.

- Policies for tardiness, missed practices or games, discipline issues.

Dear Parents:

Another basketball season is upon us. I'm excited about our team and hope your kids are, too.

My primary goal for the season is for everyone to have fun and improve their basketball skills. My basic philosophy is to foster a positive, supportive atmosphere so that every player has a great basketball experience. Regardless of ability, every member of the team deserves to be treated with encouragement and to be given equal playing time. That is to say, I'll alternate players as regularly as possible—and will not use only the better players in close games. Players should respect each other on and off the court and should learn to both win and lose well. I look to you to help reinforce these important concepts: when you come to games or practices, please limit your interaction with your children to positive encouragement from a distance. During games, please sit on the other side of the court from our team, and please treat the referees with the respect they deserve. We are our children's most important role models. I will set as good an example as I possibly can, and I would greatly appreciate your help by doing the same.

Games: Please make every effort to arrive at games 15 minutes before the scheduled start. If you know that getting your child to a game will be difficult, we can carpool. If your child cannot make it to a game, please let me know in advance. If your child misses practice the week before the game without a good reason, he or she might not play in the game. Please know that I have this policy so that participation in the games is fair for everyone.

Cancellation: Unless you hear otherwise, we will always have practice or games. In the case of cancellation, kids will be notified either at school or by means of the enclosed phone tree.

Must Bring: Please make sure that your child has a water bottle, basketball, court shoes, shorts, and a T-shirt. Balls and water bottles should be labeled.

We're looking forward to a great season of basketball. If you have questions or concerns, please feel free to contact me.

Thanks,

The Coach
4 Smithfield Lane
555-4007
coach@netdot.com

Open the season with a letter to parents that explains your coaching philosophy and outlines your expectations for the season.

Questions and Answers

Q. No one has volunteered to be the administrative parent for my team, and I'm feeling completely overwhelmed. What do I do?

A. Delegating a parent to be team manager would certainly free you from having to deal with a lot of details, but if no one is willing to help, you can manage this on your own. The key will be organization. First you will need to establish the phone tree, which will free you from ever having to call more than one or two players. And you need to do the schedule for where and when to meet for games and practices. You need to take care of these two items early. Also, don't feel shy about calling parents and asking them to get involved in the administrative details. Just because no one has volunteered for the whole job, doesn't mean they wouldn't be willing to help with one or more specific projects if you ask them. Take charge and stress to them that the more they help, the better their child's season will be.

Q. Where do I find out the details of practice and game scheduling? Do I have to call the gym to arrange times or call coaches to set up games? Is this something I have to take care of myself, or does the league do it?

A. It depends on how things are set up in your town and school. If yours is a school-sponsored team, talk to the athletic director or physical education teacher. If sports are sponsored by a recreation department, the best place to start is with the recreation director. You might find that everything will be done for you, from gym time to game scheduling. It is useful to have the names and phone numbers of the other coaches in case, for example, there is ever a question of game cancellation.

There are many administrative details that every new coach needs to learn about, so if your league, recreation department, or school holds any general meetings about the season, make every effort to attend. Talk to veteran coaches, either at these meetings or on your own—they'll be an invaluable source of information.

Q. I'm having trouble drafting my letter to parents about what I expect from the season. I don't want to offend anyone, or hurt anyone's feelings, or come on too strong.

A. This doesn't have to be the Gettysburg Address—just write down what you want the kids to get out of the season, what you expect from the parents, and how excited you are to be coaching. Stress the positive. If you're worried about the tone, have someone else read it before it goes out. You can even just use our sample letter, word for word.

Q. I'm thinking about asking a girl from the local high school varsity team to assist me in coaching my girls' team. I thought she might inspire the girls and be a great role model. Is this a good idea?

A.   It is always a good idea to get help from high school or former high school players. Good role models send out all the messages that we as coaches are trying to teach. Make sure as best you can that the assistant you choose is both enthusiastic and modest. The younger kids will often imitate the high school girl. Hence, enthusiasm will breed enthusiasm, and the modest spirit of giving and teamwork will breed an unselfish attitude in the players.

Essential Skills— and How to Teach Them

The Fundamentals

Anyone who has watched a basketball game is impressed when an impossible shot touches "nothing but net," or when a player makes a great steal or an even better save. But underneath the flash and thrill of exciting basketball moves is the time spent working on the less glamorous but infinitely important fundamentals of dribbling, passing, catching, pivoting, shooting, and rebounding. The best players are those who have mastered—and always keep working on—the basics of the game. Your job as coach is to help your players understand and practice the fundamentals to give them a solid skills foundation.

A coach demonstrates proper dribbling form.

Dribbling

While there are many skills that players need to play the game, the most important in the development of a basketball player is dribbling. It is a skill that should be developed first and worked on during all practice situations. The greater the improvement in dribbling, also known as ball handling, the more confident the player will become. Dribbling is also a portable skill: it can be practiced anywhere you find a ball and a surface suitable for bouncing it. In addition, dribbling is an activity that is conducive to learning while your players are having fun and keeping moving.

The Principles

There are five beginning principles that make a successful dribbler:

1. **Fingertip control.** The flat part of the fingertips, the last inch or so of the fingers, is what should touch the ball and push it onto the floor.

2. **Staying low.** It is imperative that all skills be taught from an athletic position, which means the players' knees are bent and their bodies are flexed at the waist.

3. **Head up.** Players should keep their heads up, especially when practicing stationary dribbling. The ball is round, the floor is flat—the ball will come back up to the hand. Players need to develop confidence that the ball will consistently bounce off the floor and back to their hands. Players have to dribble while looking up in order to "see the court" and exploit opportunities.

4. **Either hand.** Players need to learn to dribble using either hand. It is important to start players at a young age practicing dribbling using the nonpreferred hand as much as the preferred hand.

5. **Protect the ball.** Players must learn to shield the ball with their bodies so defenders cannot steal it.

Teaching the Technique

One of the most effective ways to teach the five fundamental principles of dribbling is first to explain these principles and then to ask the players how much they remember. Pull out a chair in front of the group, sit in it, and dribble. Have your players coach you. Ask them questions: Am I low? Is my head up? Do I have fingertip control? The players learn that they can practice the proper fundamentals sitting down, not just in game-playing situations. (And if they were to walk into a gym of serious basketball players, they would observe that the players who were not on the court were sitting on the sidelines bouncing balls.) Encourage your players to practice their drib-

Dribbling Skills
- five principles of a good dribble/stationary dribble
- dribbling on the move
- changing speed and direction: starting and stopping

Learning Drills and Games

The following drills and games are covered in detail in chapter 9.
- Heads-Up F6
- Crossover Move F7
- Moving Dribble F8
- Whistle F9
- Dribble Tag F10
- Steal-the-Ball F11
- Dribble Relays F12
- Stop-and-Go F13
- Full-Court Stop and Dribble F14
- Stop-and-Cross F15

bling skills from a sitting position. The key factor in learning how to dribble is to dribble. If it is at all possible, create a situation where every player has a ball to practice with.

It is important that players learn how to start and stop a dribble without traveling. To stop a dribble, the player must come to a one-two stop, where one foot will land first, or a simultaneous two-foot stop. In a one-two stop, the foot that lands first is the player's pivot foot. After a two-foot stop, either foot can be moved first, and the other foot then becomes the pivot foot. Your players should do a lot of pivoting drills so they become comfortable with the skill (see Pivoting on pages 31–32).

Passing

One of the crucial fundamentals to the game is successful passing. The strength and skills that players develop to pass effectively are the same ones they'll use for shooting and rebounding—shooting is simply an extension of passing.

The Principles

The motion of passing is simple and fluid: players step toward the target, extend their arms, snap their wrists, and follow through. A crucial element to good passing is to have good body balance—passers are always stepping toward the target, transferring strength to the ball as they release it.

A good way to remember the proper hand position for passing is to think of your hands turning inside out as you release the ball from your body out to your receiver. Picture your hands on the side of the ball. As you extend, you turn your hands so at the end of the pass your palms will face outside. You may find that your younger players with smaller hands have a harder time mastering this. They should concentrate on snapping their wrists regardless of how far the ball actually travels. It is important to emphasize good wrist and hand control from the start; as the players grow, their skills will improve.

There are four principal passes, all of which will be used extensively during game situations:

1. **Two-handed chest pass.** Players hold the ball with their fingers on the sides of the ball and their thumbs behind. Have them step to the target, extend their arms, snap their wrists, and follow through. Younger players with smaller hands can do this pass by putting one hand on top of the ball and the other hand beside it. This hand position is also used in the *triple-threat position*, a versatile stance used by both offensive and defensive players. In the triple-threat position, the player is well balanced, with weight forward on the balls of the feet, poised to move quickly into a shot, dribble, or pass.

Left: A two-handed chest pass.

Right: In the *triple-threat position*, players put one hand on top of the ball and the other hand beside it.

If your players are having difficulty forcefully "snapping" the ball away, concentrate on one-hand passing and work on pushing through to the target. This is called a *one-handed push pass*.

Some younger players lack the strength to snap the ball properly in the two-handed chest pass. They should begin with the one-handed push pass, where one hand guides the ball and the other drives the ball through to the target.

A coach demonstrates the overhead pass.

2. Bounce pass. Players hold the ball with their fingers on the sides of the ball and their thumbs behind for this pass. Have them step toward the target person and bounce the ball a little over half-way to this player, so it will be rising to the waist of this person. Bouncing it less than halfway will make the ball rise too high to meet the receiver properly; bouncing it close to the receiver's feet makes the reception too difficult.

3. Overhead pass. Players hold the ball in both hands over their heads. Have them step toward the target person, extend their arms, snap their wrists, and follow through to the target. Rebounders use this kind of pass to clear the ball without bringing it down where it might be tied up or stolen.

4. Baseball pass. As the name suggests, this is a one-handed throw, typically used for long passes, such as in the fast break when the offensive player sprints to the basket, often after a rebound. This pass can be difficult for young players, especially 6- or 7-year-olds, to do. The key to the baseball pass is for the player to turn the thumb inside when throwing the ball—this keeps the ball much straighter than if the thumb turns to the outside.

Passing Skills
- passing principles
- chest pass
- bounce pass
- overhead pass
- baseball pass

Learning Games and Drills
The following drills are covered in detail in chapter 9.
- Partner Passing F16
- Dribble Passing F17
- Pass-Receive F18

Teaching the Principles
The best way to work on passing is through two-player partner drills. Spread your players around the gym. Have one person be the receiver, the other the passer. Remind your players always to

1. step as they pass the ball
2. look at the person to whom they are passing
3. extend their arms

Catching

One of the most undertaught but critical fundamentals of the game is catching—the skill that coincides with passing the ball. While it is true that players catch the ball with their hands, they also catch the ball with their eyes. It is important for players to see the ball come into their hands: most of the problems that both experienced and novice players have in ball handling tend to stem from trying to do something before they actually have possession of the ball.

The Principles

The key to good catching is being ready to meet the pass: keeping knees bent, showing hands to the passer with palms up to give the passer a target. As the pass comes, the receiver jumps forward to meet the ball and restores his or her balance. As a player is catching the ball, a pivot foot should be established.

Players have to develop a touch and a feel for the ball, what is known as having "soft hands." Developing soft hands entails catching the ball, bringing it in to the body, and getting in a balanced position to do the next motion.

Teaching the Principles

The main components of catching are to have good balance, see the target, and meet the ball. The best way for players to catch the ball is to learn to concentrate, use their eyes, and work on the drills.

Pivoting

Learning to pivot is one of the most critical basketball fundamentals, because it is a violation for players to catch the ball and keep moving their feet. Referees aren't lenient about this (except in the NBA!). A player is able to move only one foot after catching the ball—the other foot has to stay stationary. Picture one of your shoes nailed to the floor at the toe. You can turn your foot, but you can't lift it off the floor, except to shoot or pass. Once you've lifted this foot for shooting or passing, you can't touch it down again if you still have the ball. You have to dribble *before* you move that pivot foot off the floor. Pivoting helps players establish proper balance after receiving a pass, stopping a dribble, or rebounding. When players pick up the ball and someone tries to steal it, they need to be comfortable pivoting to protect the ball. One of the reasons people who can't pivot get the ball stolen from them is that they stand straight ahead, facing the defender, who can come up and just take the ball away. But if players pivot, they can always keep part of their body between the ball and the defender.

The Principles

The keys to the pivot are good balance and establishing a legal pivot foot. Players can start a legal dribble or pass by stepping with the nonpivot foot. When players are either dribbling or about to receive the ball and they need to come to a stop, there are two different ways to do so.

Catching Skills
- catching principles
- soft hands
- anticipating the pass

Learning Drills

The following drills are covered in detail in chapter 9.
- Soft Hands **F19**
- Anticipating the Pass **F20**
- Bad Pass **F21**

Pivoting Skills
- pivoting principles
- one-two stop
- two-footed stop

Learning Drills
The following drills are covered in detail in chapter 9.
- Jump-Stop Left-Right and Right-Left F22
- Two-Footed Stop F23
- Dribbling Whistle Pivot F24
- Dribble, Jump-Stop, Pivot, Pass F25
- Combination F26

1. **One-two stop.** As its name implies, one foot hits the floor, then the other. The first foot that hits is the pivot foot. If your player is extended a bit, his body is off balance. Make sure the player keeps his first foot down, lowers his hips, and brings his second foot back into a more comfortable position. This will help him establish a strong, balanced stance. The player can then jab with that second foot in a circle all the way around the first foot.

2. **Two-footed stop.** Here both feet hit the floor at the same time. The advantage to this kind of stop is that either foot can then be the pivot foot. The two-footed stop is difficult to do if a player is going fast. Players in motion should always come to a one-two stop.

Teaching the Principles
The most effective way to teach pivoting is to get your players to feel balance. Have your team run around as a group; then blow your whistle for them to stop—you pick either a one-two stop or a two-footed stop. Ask your players if they feel on balance. Push on their shoulders—if they are on balance, with knees bent, hips low, on a solid base, they can't be knocked over. But if they are standing erect with their knees locked, they can get knocked over. Go around the group and ask them questions about their positions: Do you feel balanced? What would happen if I pushed you? Teach them how to have a properly balanced athletic position.

Shooting
Shooting is one fundamental that everyone wants to practice. There's no

The keys to proper shooting are rhythm and tempo.

question that it's a thrill to get a ball in the basket—this is what attracts everyone to the game. It's important to teach young people the proper shooting fundamentals, especially since the advent of the three-point shot, which is allowed in some youth leagues. The three-point shot is exciting and impressive, but what most young kids do is hurl the ball through the air without any of the mechanics of shooting. Although they occasionally make a three-point shot, the proper techniques are lost, and usually so is the opportunity to score. One of the responsibilities coaches have is to emphasize the proper mechanics of shooting.

The Principles

The keys to proper shooting are rhythm and tempo. The mechanics of the shot are really the same motion a player uses when dribbling and passing: pressing the fingertips down on the ball, extending and snapping them, and following through to the target. When the knees bend and then straighten, the body comes up, the ball comes up, and the arms start to extend—this is the rhythm you are trying to develop.

Teaching the Principles

The best way to teach the fundamentals of shooting is to start close to the basket. Have your players put the strong hand directly behind the ball so that they feel the pressure on the flat part of their fingers, and there is a little space between the palm and the ball. The weak hand should be placed on the side of the ball and serve as a guide hand. Players should bring their elbows back so the ball is aligned with the strong side hip, knee, and toe. The ball is now in "the pocket"—just below the waist—the strength in shooting comes from the position of the ball in tight like this and from the pop of the knees (see photo below left). Many coaches teach players to bend their knees, but you want to stress to your players that they should quickly bend their knees and then pop back up. When players' knees pop, the shooting arm extends up in the air and the guide hand directs it. As the ball comes up, the shooting wrist snaps, and the fingers should snap toward the target. Always make sure that there is a follow-through aligning the index finger, elbow, hip, and knee with the hoop.

It's fine for younger players to bring the ball lower than their waists to start the shot—it doesn't have to start up in the pocket, since they aren't

Left: When shooting, players should have the strong hand directly behind the ball, with the ball resting on the flat part of the fingers, and the weak hand placed on the side of the ball as a guide. The ball should be aligned with the strong side hip, knee, and toe.

Right: As the ball comes up, the shooting wrist snaps, and the shooting fingers should snap toward the target. Follow-through is important: the index finger, elbow, hip, and knee should all align with the hoop.

Younger players may have to hold the ball lower to shoot, but hand position and body motion are the same.

Shooting Skills
- shooting principles
- proper shot technique
- the layup
- free throws

Shooting Drills
The following drills are covered in detail in chapter 9.
- The Layup F27
- Layup Rhythm F28
- Layup Strength F29
- Pull-up F30
- Two-Line Layup F31
- Crossover Layup F32
- Combination Layup F33
- Two-Line Layup Back-Cut Drill F34
- Shooting Progression Drill F35
- Shooting Competition F36
- Free Throw Shooting F37
- Dribble Shoot Relay F38

strong enough for this. Just make sure that the shooting action is one continuous motion without any awkward jerks. The main point is to keep the ball in tight to the body, with the shooting hand behind the ball, with the ball resting on the flat part of the fingers, and with the nonshooting hand on the side for balance; to bend the knees; and to explode up to the basket, remembering that the ball has to go up in the air before it can go down through the basket.

You want young players to exaggerate the arc of the shot. Start them close to the basket so they get the feel of the ball going up in the air and dropping down through the basket. It's crucial to develop good form at a young age, even if players lack the strength to get the ball to the hoop. Form shooting without a ball is a good way for kids to learn and develop the shooting rhythm.

Different shots all involve footwork: players will need to learn to shoot on the move under a variety of circumstances. The most important and fundamental shot that a player needs to perfect is the *layup*. The term *layup* is used because the shot is taken so close to the hoop that the player doesn't have to "throw" the ball in; rather, he "lays" it up nice and easy, either on the backboard or right on the rim.

Rebounding

Rebounding, or gaining control of the ball after a missed shot, is a facet of the game that is important at both the defensive and offensive ends. If it is done well, rebounding can add tremendously to the success of a team. The keys to it involve using the body, being physical, developing an eye for a miss, and hustling.

The Principles
The main aspect in developing young kids' rebounding skills is the idea behind *boxing*, or *blocking out*. When a shot is taken, each defender should locate her man (a term used throughout this book to mean an assigned opponent that a player is to guard), make contact with her man, turn to face the basket, and push her hips back, driving the offensive player back. As the ball bounces off the rim, the player should jump up and try to seize the ball at the highest point possible.

How Long Can You Hold It?

If a player catches the ball and has a defender within 6 feet of him, he has up to 5 seconds to pass, shoot, or dribble. If he holds the ball for 5 seconds while closely guarded, it is a violation, and the defensive team would get possession. The closely guarded rule also applies to a dribbler. If a dribbler has a defender within 6 feet and dribbles for 5 seconds, it is a violation. If a dribbler backs up and gets more than 6 feet away, the count would stop. The 5-second count would also stop if the dribbler gets any part of her body by the defender toward the basket. It is legal for a player to catch the ball being closely guarded, hold it for 4 seconds, dribble the ball (still closely guarded) for 4 seconds, pick up the ball and hold it for another 4 seconds, and then pass, shoot, or dribble past the defender (or move more than 6 feet away). This would not be a violation.

Teaching the Principles

One key aspect in teaching kids how to rebound is rising and going for the ball. A lot of times kids wait for the ball to come to them. It is important to teach the actual jumping and aggression involved in rebounding. Make sure that players know the best way to get a rebound is at its highest peak. Some players need more encouragement than others to go after a rebound aggressively. Tell them this is no time to be polite. While the ball is in the air, it belongs to anyone who can get there. A good rebounder *wants* the ball. You might have a tall player who *should* be a great rebounder but always hangs back. Why? Possibly because he is afraid of doing something wrong once he has the ball. Let your kids understand that as long as they're playing hard and trying, you'll never fault them for a mistake.

On the defensive end, it is also important that you stress that each player should locate her man when a shot is taken to prevent this opponent from getting an offensive rebound. Make sure that each player makes contact with her man and boxes or blocks out this player.

It is difficult to teach offensive rebounding to young players because most of the time it involves a certain instinct. The keys to rebounding involve reading the "bounce" of a missed shot and staying aggressive.

Offensive Basics

Drills to teach your players important concepts such as position play, driving to the basket and cutting, and creating offensive formations, are covered in great detail in chapters 6 and 10. What follows in this section is a brief introduction to these concepts, and why they are so important.

The Positions

The standard basketball positions consist of two guards, two forwards, and one center.

Rebounding Skills
- boxing or blocking out
- jumping

Rebounding Drills
The following drills are covered in detail in chapter 9.
- Mirror F39
- Toss off the Backboard F40
- One-on-One Toss off the Backboard F41
- Two-on-Two Toss off the Backboard F42

1. The point guard is the court general. She dribbles the ball upcourt, announces plays, and makes at least the initial distribution of the ball to her teammates.

2. The shooting guard doesn't dribble the ball as much as the point guard, but rather is known as a more accurate outside shooter. The point guard tries to set up the shooting guard to get an open shot.

3. The forward on the wing is known as the *small forward*, since this player is usually the smaller of the two forwards.

4. The forward on the post is known as the *power forward*, since this player is usually the larger of the two forwards.

   The two forwards have some versatility between playing away from the basket and playing near and underneath the basket. Forwards are generally bigger than guards and do not handle the ball as much.

5. The center is normally the tallest player on the court. She plays near to the basket or in a post position. The post positions fall on the two edges of the lane: a low-post position is close up under the basket, at the base of the foul lane; a high-post position is out at the free throw line. The center's primary responsibilities on the offense are inside moves, layups, and rebounding. On defense she rebounds, blocks shots, and in general makes it harder for the opposing team to get easy, close-in baskets.

Determining Your Players' Positions

When you're deciding how to assign players to positions, have the kids perform basic ball-handling drills, both with and without defensive pressure. Determine who can use both hands effectively, who can run and dribble, who can shield the ball with their body, and who can keep their eyes up and looking while dribbling. See which players have skills that would mesh well with the various positions. The point guard position could be a prearranged position assigned by the coach, and everybody else has to fill a spot. Or it could be whoever has the ball, and everybody else has to fill a spot. Keep in mind—and make clear to your players—that playing a position doesn't mean that the player is confined to a particular spot on the floor, just a side of the floor. In fact, all offenses include a significant amount of movement that might find any player at any spot on the court at any given time.

   If you're coaching kids who have played the game before, you may find they know the positions they're used to playing and are generally well-suited to those positions. But not always. For example, if you have a player who considers himself to be a guard, but who is somewhat tall and has difficulty handling the ball, he ought to be moved to a forward or center position (nearer to the basket and guarding taller opponents). Similarly, if you have a player who plays near to the basket, but she is a skilled ball-handler and is not particularly tall, move her to the guard position. It is important to realize that a position does not restrict a player to a certain place on the floor, particularly on offense. Finally, identify the positions in which you need help and then try to fill them with the most appropriate players you have.

Driving to the Basket and Cutting

The Principles

As younger players develop a greater feel for and are more secure with dribbling, they can do drills that combine the other skills you teach them. The next step is to develop offensive moves. Now is the time to give names to moves so that younger players can associate and identify with them. You have already taught your players the cross-over move by putting their hand to the outside of the ball and crossing over to the other hand. Players should be really encouraged to *drive to the basket*, dribbling the ball to the basket with speed and energy. When there's space available and they can beat the person who is guarding them, your players should always be encouraged to drive.

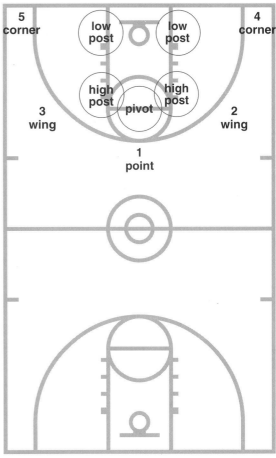

Formations (see also diagram key on page 100).

Cutting involves learning how to move on the basketball court with and without the ball. Basketball is a sport played at angles. This is one of the most important concepts to teach young players. Playing the game at angles—learning to move strategically—is crucial. There are times on the court where everyone is standing around on the offensive end, and there are other times where everyone is moving but crowding the ball, creating havoc. The best way to avoid this is by introducing proper movement without the ball. There is a series of cuts and motions that break down the proper spacing between teammates.

When there's space available and players can beat the person who is guarding them, encourage them to drive to the basket.

The ideas behind getting open are based on certain angles that are crucial in learning how to move without the ball. For example, when a player has the ball, a teammate should take two steps to the ball and then go in a straight line to the basket, creating an angle on the cut. If I wanted to receive a pass, I should take two steps to the basket and then come back at an angle to free myself.

Teaching the Principles

Teaching players how to move on the court and drive to the basket is easiest through two-man options, where one player has the ball, the other doesn't. Say Player A has the ball at the top of the circle (in the middle of the court), and Player B is at the wing (to the right or the left of Player A). If Player A dribbles at Player B, B has several cutting options to get open to receive Player A's pass.

Back-Cut to Layup. Player B takes a step toward Player A, then cuts to the basket. If he's being closely guarded he may have freed himself for a layup. The ball should be bounce-passed. **03**

Screen to Handoff. If Player A dribbles at Player B and Player B keeps coming, that means she wants to use Player A as a screener (to screen means to jump in the path of the defender). Player B comes right up to Player A, shoulder to shoulder, and Player A could just hand her the ball and Player B could continue to the basket for a layup. She could also step behind and take a shot.

Runaround. If there is a defender between Player A and Player B and she can't get the hand off, Player B should go around the person with the ball and then cut to the basket to receive either an overhead pass or a bounce pass. Going to the basket this way is called the *run around*.

Give-and-Go. The concept of give-and-go is really explained by its name: if I give you the ball, you give it back to me as I cut to the basket.

The Ten Basics

Defense
1. Sprint back
2. Know who you are guarding: point to your man and call out her number
3. Play your man in relation to the ball
4. See the ball
5. Help stop the ball

Offense
1. During a fast break, sprint the floor
2. If a teammate is open, pass to him
3. If you can beat your defender, drive to the basket
4. Free your teammates: set a screen
5. Have fun

The Basic Ingredients of a Good Team

The components of a good team can be broken down into two categories, offense and defense. The keys to a good offense are geared to the development of the fundamentals that we discuss and work on throughout the book. Good offensive teams handle the ball well, pass it well, and know how to free themselves and their teammates. Good defense begins with having good transitions, meaning sprinting down the floor and allowing no easy layups. A successful defensive team guards the ball well, has a good understanding of help defense, and contests all shots, meaning they get a hand up on a player who is taking shots. The whole book is about the development of offensive and defensive fundamentals, geared to the youth level.

Again, the principle of moving at angles or taking two steps away from where we want to go before we get there, is absolutely the same.

Pass and Screen Away. Pass and screen away uses three players (or two players and a coach) and is designed to free a teammate without the ball, so that the player will become open to receive a pass. In this play, rather than doing a give-and-go, Player A passes away from Player B and sets a screen for him (getting between his teammate and the defender).

Pick and Roll. Pick and roll is a play designed to help free a person with the ball so that player can either drive to the basket for a layup, or pass to another open player. One player sets a *pick*, another name for a screen, and then rolls toward the basket either to free her teammate to shoot or to receive a pass.

These cutting options teach players how to move with a purpose on the court and show them that they'll always have options available and choices to make, based on the situation. Later on, as the players develop, they'll be able to read the defense and determine what the path is that would be most productive or most successful for them. At this early level, you're teaching them how to move, how to play in an area, and how to play a two-man game.

Formations

You'll probably have a boy or a girl on your team who is taller than everybody else. It might be tempting to place that taller player right next to the basket and feed shots to them. While that certainly may be a recipe for scoring success, it's not teaching everybody the fundamentals of the game and not helping all of your players develop their skills. Your best bet is to keep that basket area open and encourage scoring through skills development: driving, give-and-go (see **06**), passing and cutting, and the two-man action.

To accomplish this, you need to create space on the court through *formations*. The best way to teach the game at a young level is from a three-two formation, which means a point, two wings, and two corners. From this wide-spaced formation you can practice all of the skills and plays talked

Offensive Skills

- shot and pass takes
- driving to the basket
- give-and-go
- pass and screen away
- formations
- defensive transition

Offensive Drills

The following drills are covered in detail in chapter 10.

about earlier with virtually no limits. This formation teaches your players the concept of space on the court, lets them use their choices, and encourages the dribbling techniques that they learned to drive to the basket. It also gives everybody a chance to handle the ball, since you can change positions whenever you need to.

With the three-two formation, you have many possibilities for minigames to take place at the same time. You can break down the team into one-on-one, two-on-two, or three-on-three games where fewer people are playing, so they all have more chances to get the ball. You will still be working on the whole offense, whether you start the ball in the wing and the corner on the two-on-two, or you start it from the point to the wing. Here are some suggestions for working on initial skills through minigames in a three-two formation:

- Give and go from point to wing, where point is the top of the circle, the wings are on the side.
- Give and go from the wing to the corner, where the wing cuts to the basket.
- Pass and screen away.
- Pass and screen on the ball from point to wing.
- Pass and screen on the ball from wing to corner.
- Dribble handoff, creating a two-man game off the dribble by dribbling from point to wing or by dribbling from wing to corner.

Zone Offense

If I were in charge of youth basketball leagues, I would encourage all coaches to teach the fundamentals of player-to-player defense, and in the process, everyone could work on the fundamentals of good player-to-player offense. However, many youth coaches teach zone defense, and because of this a team needs to have a zone offense in order to be able to attack this defense properly. In player-to-player defense, players guard players. In a zone defense, defensive players guard a certain area. To attack a zone defense properly, the players must have good spacing to spread the zone and must move the ball quickly to make the zone work to cover their areas.

There are two basic concepts to a zone offense: you want to form an offensive triangle, and you want to move the ball quickly. In a zone offense, ball movement is more critical than player movement. Against a man-to-man defense, you want your players moving and cutting and driving. Against the zone, you want the ball to move.

Beating the Press

Sometimes your opponents will choose to play full-court defense: that means that they will play defense on the ball right away and not wait until

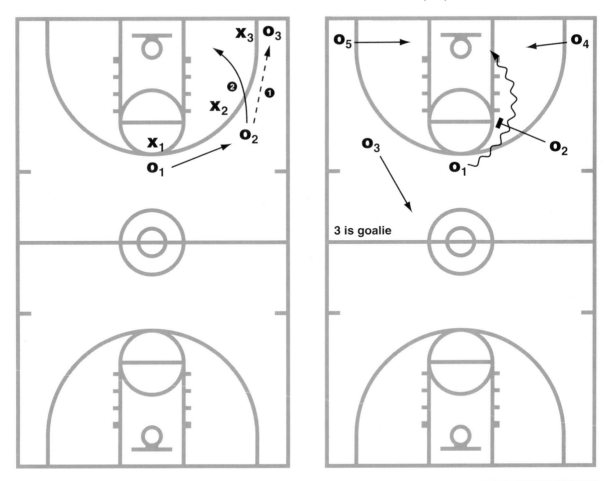

3 is goalie

your team brings the ball across the midcourt line. This is attacking with what is called a *full-court press*. (Some leagues do not allow this.) To combat a full-court press, organization and sprinting are critical components. The keys are to attack the defense, dribble up quickly, and go for an easy score. We discuss this in Beating the Press, **O20** .

Above Left: Give-and-Go from the Wing to the Corner.

Above Right: Defensive Balance. See also the diagram key on page 100.

Defensive Transition

The goal of the offense is to score: the easiest way to score is to beat the opponents down the floor and get a good shot before they are ready to defend. This is called a *fast break*. Conversely, you want to make sure that your team, no matter what age you're coaching, limits the other team's fast-break opportunities by always sprinting down the floor. Whenever you practice any of the five-on-five activities in the three-two formation, when someone drives to the basket, someone else has to be drifting back to get ready for defensive balance, just as a goalie stays near his team's goal to protect it.

You need to teach your players that an important part of working

Leave the Zone Alone

You're in a game situation: a good player from the other team is carving up your defense by driving to the basket, and your players have forgotten everything you've taught them about helping each other on the court. The game is a disaster, and the next practice you're tempted to ditch the whole player-to-player idea and just tell your team to go to a zone defense in every situation.

I don't believe in zone defenses in youth basketball, although many leagues allow them. There are many zones that coaches use. The certain alignment of players is the reason for the names of zones, including two-three, one-three-one, and three-two. When teaching zone defenses, coaches teach defending area, and the players are expected to know what area they are to cover whenever the ball is passed or dribbled.

My advice is *Stop!* Don't abandon your player-to-player defense. You are here to teach your kids some sound basketball fundamentals, and defense is the most important one. Kids are willing and enthusiastic learners as long as their teachers are, too. Go back to the basics of pressuring the ball and help and recover, and you will have a strong defensive team. Do the mirror drill every day to build up your players' enthusiasm and pride—get them yelling, "Defense!" Use the shell drills to let them learn for themselves when to help and recover and how to communicate with each other on the court. By working on their defensive skills through the above drills at every practice, and by making it fun and rewarding, your players will learn this most important facet of the game.

together and playing together involves thinking about protecting their own basket even as they are scoring on the other team's basket. This is a concept that has to be taught at a young age because mastering the *defensive transition* (being a goalie, getting back on defense, or whatever term you want to use with your team) will greatly enhance your team's chances for success on the court (see pages 41 and 137).

While you don't designate who the "goalie" is, most of the time it's the point guard because she is the one able to get back on defense quickest. It can be the weak-side wing when a shot goes up on the strong side, and the weak-side wing is in a good position to get back on defense. (We'll talk more about *strong side* and *weak side* later in this chapter on pages 45–47). For the moment, think of a line between the two baskets. If there are three or more defensive players on the left side of that imaginary line, that's the strong side. The defense will usually sag toward the "ball side," so the ball side and strong side are usually the same. Overall, the whole team needs to be aware of getting back on defense. It's a skill that needs to be developed through communication and reading the teammates.

Defensive Basics

How important is defense to the game? Consider this: basketball is played with five people on a team. If your team has the ball for half the game and the game lasts for 32 minutes, the most your team will have the ball is for 16 minutes out of that game. If you are a player on the team and only play half the game, that cuts down the amount of time you might have possession to 8 minutes. If there are five people on your team and you're sharing the ball equally, you will actually have possession of the ball for 1 or 2 minutes per game. But you'll be on defense five times as long. The entire time you aren't in possession of the ball, you are on defense. That's why teaching your players good defensive skills is one of the most crucial aspects of the game and will be a big factor in how successful you are as a team.

Defense is the one aspect of basketball that everyone has the potential to play, regardless of talent or age level. Not all of your players are going to be able to do all the skills that you ask them to do—you'll have some kids who are stronger players than others, and some players who are just better athletes. These are the kids who will shine on offense. One of the nicest aspects of teaching your players defense is that everyone has a job to do every second, and everyone can be good at it and make a strong contribution to the team.

By doing the defensive drills, you are developing a defensive philosophy. You are doing things with enthusiasm and are getting the players excited and focused on the skills they are learning. You are also teaching them to hustle, and you are setting a tone and atmosphere that defense is fun.

Defensive Stance

The first key to moving defensively on the court is to learn the defensive stance. The easiest way to teach the proper stance position is through a mirror drill, where your players will mirror you or an assistant standing in the front of the group to demonstrate. Have your players stand with their feet wider than shoulder width apart, knees deeply bent. They should be well

Left: Mirror drills, in which players mirror your movements as you hold the ball, develop proper defensive stance.

Right: As an alternative to mirror drills, players can pair off to practice tracing the ball.

Defensive Skills

- defensive stance
- tracing the ball
- defensive slide
- defending the basket
- denying the pass
- help and recover
- help-side defense
- communicating the defensive transition

Defensive Drills

The following drills are covered in detail in chapter 11.

- Stance **D1**
- Quick Hands, Quick Feet **D2**
- Mirror **D3**
- Dick Harter **D4**
- Zigzag **D5**
- Figure 8 **D6**
- Containing the Dribbler **D7**
- One-on-One Full-Court **D8**
- Person-to-Person Full-Court **D9**
- Two-on-Two **D10**
- The Shell **D11**
- Two-on-Two Shell **D12**
- Four-on-Four Shell **D13**
- Help and Recover **D14**
- Help and Rotation **D15**
- Three-on-Three Stop Game **D16**
- Combination Transition **D17**

(continues next page)

Double-Teaming

Double-teaming is a defensive tactic where two players guard one player, generally the one with the ball. It can be an effective way to steal the ball or prevent the offensive player from driving in for a shot or passing up the court. There are many ways to double-team. You could double-team the dribbler as she comes across the midcourt line. It is common in younger leagues to have a defender who is guarding a weaker player leave her man and go double-team a better player. Some teams will wait until a pass is made and then double-team the player who receives the pass. It is equally common in youth leagues to prohibit double-teaming, especially in the younger age groups, precisely because it can wreak such havoc on an offense.

balanced and solid, with their weight on the front of their feet, not on their toes. Tell them that if someone tried to slip a piece of paper underneath the heels, they could do so. Their weight should be on the inside of the feet, so they are ready to move, ready to lunge out to either side.

Learning to trace the ball is vital for good defense because a defender's hands will often be mirroring the movements of the offense's ball.

Defensive Slide

Your players have to be ready to move in any direction the offense goes. This is where the *defensive slide* comes in. Players need to be in a good defensive stance, balanced, with one foot slightly ahead of the other. Picture defensive sliding as a race between the front foot and the back foot, where the back foot never catches the front. There's always a space in between. A coach should be able to point in any direction and have the kids slide their lead foot in that direction, with the back foot quickly trailing, repeating the motion. As your players move their feet, they need to stay low in their stance position and keep their heads and shoulders level, without bouncing up and down. They also need to be ready to change direction. They do this by keeping the back foot down and swinging the front foot around. This move is called a *drop step*. Most of the time in a defensive stance players are going sideways and backward and need the drop step to defend change-of-direction moves like the crossover.

Defending the Ball

The defender should be one arm's length away from the offensive player. The defender should always have her hand up, tracing the ball and almost, but not quite, touching it when the dribbler is holding the ball. As the player with the ball dribbles, the defender slides her feet and moves her hands. If the offense picks up the ball, both the defenders' hands are up, smothering the ball. The defender doesn't need space between her and the ball now because the offensive player has picked up the ball and can't dribble anymore. If the offensive player goes to shoot, the defender raises one hand up, yells, "Shot!" and tries to block it.

Minor Injuries? Think RICE

Bumps and bruises are a part of youth sports. If your player's injury needs more attention than the following, be sure to contact your local emergency room or physician. For minor sprains and strains, however, the RICE method will help a minor soft tissue injury heal faster.

Relative Rest. Avoid activities that exacerbate the injury, but continue to move the injured area gently. Early gentle movement promotes healing.

Ice. Apply ice to the affected area for 20 minutes; then leave it off for at least an hour. Do not use ice if you have circulatory problems.

Compression. Compression creates a pressure gradient that reduces swelling and promotes healing. An elastic bandage provides a moderate amount of pressure that will help discourage swelling.

Elevation. Elevation is especially effective when used in conjunction with compression. Elevation provides a pressure gradient: the higher the injured body part is raised, the more fluid is pulled away from the injury site via gravity. Elevate the injury as high above the heart as comfortable. Continue to elevate intermittently until swelling is gone.

Defending against a Fast Break

First demonstrate how a player on defense should never be beaten by an offensive player—no matter what, the defense should run to catch up. Guard a player and have him get a step by you and start to speed dribble to the basket. Show how to turn and run to catch up with a player making a fast break—don't do a defensive slide, but instead chase the offensive player right to the basket area as fast as possible, knowing that in a game the defensive player will get some help from his teammates.

Defending the Basket

I'm a big believer in defending the basket area first and making that area look like it has a lot of people. We do this with a simple philosophy of dividing the court in half. You can tell your players that you have just painted an imaginary line down the middle of the floor, from basket to basket down the center of the court. You will use this imaginary line as a reference point. The side of the floor that the ball is on is called the *ball side*; the side of the floor that the ball is not on is called the *help side* or *weak side*.

When guarding the dribbler, the defender should always have a hand up, tracing the ball.

Be Alert to Health Problems

There's nothing more frightening for a parent—or coach—than to see a child in distress and not know what to do. Breathing problems, including exercise-induced asthma, are more prevalent in children than ever before. Make sure that you talk to parents about how important it is for you to be aware of any pre-existing physical condition that any of your players may have. In addition, parents need to give you as much information as possible about what to do if their child is in distress and who to contact if problems occur. Forewarned is forearmed.

The Principles

The point of defense is to stop the ball from going into the basket. Defenders' initial positions change whenever the ball is passed. If the ball is passed from one side of the floor to the other, the help-side players become ball-side defenders, and the ball-side players become help-side defenders. Players are constantly moving and adjusting the relationship. How a defender plays his man is always dependent upon where the ball is and where the man is.

Ball-Side Defense: Denying the Pass

If a defensive player is guarding an offensive player without the ball on the ball side and the offensive player is closer to the basket than the ball is, the defensive player should try to *deny the pass*. This means the defender tries to stop the offensive player from receiving a pass. The defending player

When guarding an offensive player who is well placed to receive a pass, the defender should assume the *deny position*: she should be able to see the ball and the likely receiver simultaneously, while keeping a hand and foot in the passing line, the line the ball would travel if a pass were made to the offensive player. Here the coach demonstrates the deny position.

should get into the deny position: in a defensive stance, she turns and looks out to the side so she can see the ball and her man at the same time, while keeping a hand and foot in the *passing line*, the line the ball would draw through the air from passer to receiver. This is called the *deny position*.

Ball-Side Defense: Help and Recover

If a defensive player is guarding a person who is farther away from the basket than the ball—for example, outside the three-point line—and the person with the ball is at the foul line, the defensive player is in a *help position*, where he should be helping the ball—that is, helping to stop the ball from getting closer to the basket.

This means that the defensive player leaves his own man to stop the ball, since his man is less important than the ball is right now. Once the defensive player helps stop the ball on the ball side, he goes back to, or *recovers* to, his own man—the player he was guarding. This move is known as a *help and recover* and is a vital defensive move. The point of help and recover is for your players to learn that they aren't always going to stick with the player they are guarding, regardless of the situation. They will need to learn how to read the play, to see where the ball is, where the offensive players are, communicate their moves to their own teammates, and respond.

Help-Side Defense

Whenever a player is guarding someone on the help side—the side of the court without the ball—she should be in a good *help-side* or *weak-side help position*: with one foot extending over that invisible line dividing the court into the ball side and the help side, she stays low, points to the ball with one hand and to her man with the other, and looks straight out so she can see both. She needs to be ready to switch to a ball-side defense as soon as the ball is passed.

A defender on the help side should straddle the invisible line between the help side and ball side of the court and should keep in view both the ball and the player being covered, while extending one arm toward each.

Communicating the Defense

Not only is communication vital to a good defense, but it also builds energy and enthusiasm. If a player is guarding someone who doesn't have the ball, and the ball is passed out to this opponent, the player should get into a good defensive stance, yell, "Ball!" and start to trace the ball with one hand.

Key to Success: End a Defensive Session with Enthusiasm

After your team has worked on a defensive block, really emphasize the good work they have done. Bring the group in and have the players put their hands into the circle. When the coach yells, "On three! One, two, three!" the whole team should say, "Defense!" Learning defense takes a lot of hard work on the part of both you and your players—but defense can also be quickly improved with a sound foundation. It is up to you to keep your players excited and enthusiastic and to take pride in sprinting the floor, getting in their stance, and communicating. Meeting to give a team cheer for defense is a great way to reinforce all the hard work everyone has put in.

Defensive Summary

Here's a nutshell summary of defense to give your players:

"If your man is closer to the basket than the ball, don't let him get the ball. You deny him the ball. If your man is farther away from the basket than the ball is, then you help stop the ball. If you're on the help side, maintain a weak-side help position: keep one foot in the lane, on the ball side of the court. Stay low, with one hand toward the ball and the other toward your man, and look straight out so you can see both. Every time you switch positions, yell what it is now so that you and your teammates know what is going on and what needs to happen next."

On defense, every defender has the responsibility to stop the ball from getting too close to the basket. Whenever a defender is beaten, someone else must leave the player she is guarding to stop the ball before it gets to the basket. Once the opposing playing who is driving stops and picks up her dribble, whoever helped should recover to the original player that she was guarding. It is also the team's responsibility to get the rebound once the ball is shot. Every player should try to make contact with his man and then go get the ball. Making contact with the player you are guarding when the ball is shot is called *boxing* or *blocking out*.

That tells her teammates she knows her responsibility and is ready to play. The players who were on the help side now know they are help-side defenders, so they yell, "Weak-side help! Weak-side help!"

Similarly, you are bound to play teams that will set screens, either on the ball or for each other. It's sound offense. The easiest and most effective way to communicate the screens is to try to talk them out by yelling, "Screen coming!" Your players also need to be ready to move when someone gets caught in a screen, and they need to communicate with each other while they are doing it. This is called the *jump switch*: when one player gets caught in a screen, whoever is guarding the screen should jump out and yell, "Switch!" This will help your other players know what is going on and what needs to happen next. The team is communicating their jobs and positions, which keeps everyone aware of where they should be on the court, and it also gives them energy and enthusiasm for the job they now have to accomplish.

Talk Out Your Transitions

When your players switch from offense to defense, they need to communicate with each other *before* they get to the other end of the court so that they address potential problems before such situations happen. As soon as the ball is turned over, your players need to take the initiative and yell, "I'll take number 6!" or "I'll take 99!" or they let their teammates know who is going to cover whom, so that they don't run down to the other end of the court all trying to cover the same opponent, leaving other players open. Teach them that as soon as there is a transition they should pick a player, tell their teammates whom they are covering, and then zero in on that player so that their transitions are both quick and effective.

Turnovers: When You Lose Possession, *Sprint!*

One of the most important skills you need to drill into your players is that whenever they lose posses-sion of the ball—if it's stolen, if it's a violation, if they take a shot and miss the rebound, or if they make a basket—they should *sprint* to the other end of the court. Make sure you emphasize this throughout your practices, reminding your players over and over again to sprint to the other end. If you do, you'll find that when it comes to a game, they will automatically move and move and move. All your hard work will pay off.

The Shell Drill

The foundation of our defense is really in the shell drill. The shell or box set is a defensive formation you can use for a wide variety of drills, including one-on-one, two-on-two, three-on-three drills, and so on. In a typical two-on-two shell drill, two defenders guard two offensive wings while the coach dribbles down the center. As the coach advances and the position of the ball becomes more important, defenders leave the wings. As the coach passes to the wings, and the wings then return the ball, defenders develop the defensive moves they'll need during a game, including moving from ball-side to help-side positions, help and recovery, and learning to commu-nicate with their teammates. By learning to play defense in this setup, your players learn to communicate, to stay in their stance, and to jump as the ball moves. With a four-on-four drill, you can also teach how to defend against cutters and screens. We'll explore defensive sets in greater detail in chapter 11.

CHAPTER 5

The Practice

Preparation Is Key

The single most important factor for successful practices, and especially for the first day of practice, is to *be prepared*. Have your practice plan organized and ready to go before you leave for the gym. Don't plan on spending a few minutes before practice coming up with a practice plan—kids will often come to the gym early, and you'll need to be ready for them.

Be Early

Always plan to arrive at the gym at least 10 minutes before practice starts, and from 20 to 30 minutes before practice on the first day. Get the equipment ready if the gym is available. You're bound to have some players come early, and they can use this time to practice dribbling and shooting. On the first day you can use the time to introduce yourself to the players and parents individually and get to know how the kids move on the court. Parents will often approach you with questions before practice once the season is underway.

Get Them to Respond to You Immediately

At exactly the time practice is supposed to start, walk to the center of the court and blow your whistle. Your players will almost certainly meander in your direction this first practice. Explain to them how happy you are to be there and what a good-looking group they are, but that they've got to learn good habits right away. When the whistle blows, everyone should get into the circle with energy and enthusiasm. So send them out again, and then bring them back in with your whistle. This time they should all run into the circle. Make a big deal of it—tell them, "Great job. You should do that every time." For more information and advice about establishing good habits in your players, see Creating an Atmosphere of Good Habits in chapter 1.

Learn Their Names

The first practice is an intimidating time for your players. A good way to make them feel at ease and also to reinforce that you're in charge and in control of the situation is for you to know their names right away. It is unbelievably rewarding for a kid to meet someone in authority for the first time and have that person call him or her by name, to know that "Hey, the coach noticed me." Have your players introduce themselves—go around the circle and have each player say his or her name. Explain that because you really want to learn all of their names right away, throughout the practice you're going to point your finger at different players, who should tell you their names, no matter what is going on. And then look at a person and point your finger to show them how you want the players to respond.

All through practice, from the opening group talk through the drills and to the end huddle, stop suddenly, point at different people, and learn their names. By the end of practice you'll know every player's name on your team. It's important to the kids to be recognized by their own name, and it's a great way to immediately bond with your team.

Format for Practice

It is essential to have a consistent format for every practice. Like all routines, when you set up a structure for practices it helps in many ways—it gets the kids into habits and gets them into a good pattern where they know what to expect. It will also help you down the line to establish when the next activity should start. There should be flexibility within the routine, but the structure really should remain consistent. Make sure to allow for a couple of water breaks.

Key to Success: The Discovery Method

One of the most effective ways of teaching children a skill is to use the *discovery method*—where they discover the answer for themselves. Here's how it works: you give your players a demonstration of the technique you want them to do. For example, if you wanted to teach them how to dribble the ball properly, instead of saying, "This is the part of the hand you should use to dribble the ball," say instead, "Watch this. You tell me which part of my hand I'm using when I dribble. Where is my head? Where am I looking?" Let your players tell you what is going on with the drill, so they explain it to you.

Set up the drill, and then ask players to identify what you're looking for. Bring out the dialogue from them. As long as they are consistent with the words they use, they can make up their own basketball vocabulary that works for all of you. It's important that your team develops its own vocabulary. The key point is that everyone understands the vocabulary you'll be using and that you all discover it together.

The great thing about the discovery method is that everyone is concentrating on what is in front of them. You ask players the question before the demonstration so you are leading them to the important concept of the skill, but they discover it for themselves. Everyone has a much greater chance of remembering something they discover for themselves rather than something they are told.

Preparation is the single greatest factor in successful practices. Always plan practice sessions in advance. A practice worksheet, broken down according to the elements of the practice, is an excellent planning tool.

Practice Session Worksheet

Team Meeting

_____
_____
_____
_____
_____
_____

Warm-Up/Fundamentals

_____
_____
_____
_____
_____
_____
_____
_____

Offense/Defense

_____
_____
_____
_____
_____
_____
_____

Fun Ending Activity

_____
_____
_____
_____
_____

Wrap-Up/Doggy Bag

_____
_____
_____
_____
_____

The following format template is for 90-minute practice sessions. If you have less or more practice time, you can adjust the individual segments according to your needs.

- team meeting: 5 minutes
- warm-up: 10 minutes
- fundamentals: 20 minutes
- defense: 20 minutes
- offense: 20 minutes
- fun, ending activity/scrimmage: 10 minutes
- wrap-up/doggy bag: 5 minutes

A brief overview of these components is given here. See chapter 6 for the specifics.

Team Meeting (5 minutes)

Many of your players will get to the court early. Make sure you have balls available for them to shoot baskets, practice skills, and play the game. Always start practice promptly. Call your team together for their group meeting, which should last only about 5 minutes. Now is the time to tell your players what skills you'll be emphasizing during practice—it gives them something specific to concentrate on throughout practice and provides a focus for each individual session.

Warm-Up (10 minutes)

Young players don't need much stretching, so you can go right into a variety of warm-up exercises that will get them moving immediately, involved in what they are doing, and having fun.

Fundamentals (20 minutes)

The game of basketball is based on the fundamentals of dribbling, passing, catching, pivoting, shooting, and rebounding. A solid skills foundation is essential. Young players will always need to work on their ball-handling skills and will be working on them throughout practice. It is good to start the practice with a review of skills and drills to reinforce good ball-handling techniques that they can practice as they move through the other segments.

Every practice should have a short review of passing techniques and some passing drills. The kids enjoy these drills and feel they are mastering skills quickly, and they can always use the practice. As with dribbling, your players will be using their passing skills throughout practice as they learn offensive and defensive skills. Shooting games and drills are also fun for the kids and should be part of every practice.

Offense/Defense (20 minutes each)

The defensive and offensive blocks will be where you'll spend much of your time and energy at practice, at first teaching the skills through drills and then practicing and honing them over and over. Keep the kids moving, and make the drills competitive and gamelike—you'll be surprised at how quickly the kids learn the drills, the concepts, and the skills needed to play a good game.

Ending Activity (10 minutes)

It's important to make the end of practice a fun time—your players have worked hard on learning some fairly complicated concepts in the last two blocks, so end practices with something that is both competitive and rewarding. You can always do an activity that helps tie together the skills you've concentrated on learning that day, and scrimmaging will be a good choice, especially as your players improve. This is a good time for you to get involved and be a part of the game as well.

Wrap-Up/Doggy Bag (5 minutes)

Always end your practice with a group meeting, giving a quick summary of what you did, praising what your players did well, and commenting on what they need to work on. Kids like the idea of being given a project to work on when they aren't at practice. Take something out of the session that needs work and give it as homework. Most kids don't like the word "homework," so call it their "doggy bag" since it is something to take home with them. This is a good way to get them to practice skills that are difficult for them, and it keeps them involved with the sport when they aren't at practice.

Practice Success

Make Sure They're Listening

Even though you can tell your team 20 times that listening is important, your actions will speak louder than your words. Talk to them about how important it is to listen, that when you're talking you don't want others talking, and that you want them to look at you. Then tell them you're going to give them a test to see how well they listen. Say that when you blow the whistle, everyone should get up to begin practice, and then explain what you'll do—warm-up, then agility drills, then foot fire, for example. So you tell them "When the whistle blows, everybody up." And then say, "Okay, up!" and don't blow the whistle. You'll see at least half the team will jump up. Either say, "Aha!" or don't say anything. Let them figure out why some are sitting and some are standing. Then when they sit down, say, "Oops, some of us weren't really listening," and then blow the whistle—and everybody's up facing you. This is an effective way to get your players to realize that when you say you want them to listen to what you're saying, you really want them to *hear* what you're saying.

Keep Your Players Moving

Young kids have incredibly high energy levels—they run everywhere. As a coach, you will need to give them activities that take into account this high level of energy and that provide immediate positive reinforcement. Break up explanations and drills into segments: briefly explain the drill and then let players try it right away. The drills in this book are designed so that the most number of players can participate at once, and you should always be conscious of not letting players stand around for any length of time. In drills that leave some players on the sidelines, use these kids as "timekeepers," "ball boys and girls," or "managers"—give them jobs. Divide into small groups and use all those baskets at once.

Scrimmage

How important is it to scrimmage during every practice? This is a matter of personal preference for each coach. I view most of the drills that we discuss as a form of scrimmaging, just broken down into smaller groups of two on two or three on three. In this sense a large proportion of each practice is devoted to minigames. Early in the season, this can be more useful when the kids are just getting underway. Once you are into the season, five-on-five scrimmages become more important, and it's always a great ending activity.

Encourage Politeness

It's important that your team knows that when you're talking to one individual, you're really talking to the whole team. While you might be addressing one particular player about a technique, everybody should be listening at that time. A good way to keep the group organized and not have kids coming and going, some sitting down and some standing up, is to have all the players who aren't involved in an individual drill or scrimmage stand at the sideline, either underneath the basket or along the sideline, watching the action. You want them to maintain their attention on what the team is doing or what the coach is trying to teach.

Players should also know that when you are giving them help with a technique or skill, it's not a two-way conversation. If you say something like, "Hey, Jimmy, you've got to move out of the 3-second area. You've been in there too long. The ref's going to call 3 seconds," he shouldn't engage in a dialogue about it—your wish is his command. You are the sole authority figure at practice, and you should make this clear to all of your players.

Keep Them Hydrated

Your players are going to be working hard, and it is important they don't get dehydrated. Notice how much they are sweating. There will always be a kid who really sweats a lot, and chances are that child needs a lot of water. Build water breaks into the practice schedule and make sure they're all getting a drink. Two water breaks in 90 minutes is a good rule of thumb.

Reading the Diagrams

Each diagram in this book is designed to make it easier to understand both the fundamental concepts of the skills and the accompanying drills. Refer to the court terminology diagram (page 13) and diagram key (page 96). Each offensive player is labeled with an "O" and a number; the corresponding defensive player is labeled with an "X" and the same number. The ball is depicted as a dot. When a player passes the ball, it is depicted as a dotted line. When the player dribbles, it is depicted as a wavy line. Arrows will indicate direction. Complicated drills may be explained with more than one diagram.

Encourage the players to come with their own water bottles to avoid a traffic jam at the water fountain (this goes for both practices and games). Water bottles should be labeled with their names.

Help Your Players to Speak Up

It's really important that kids are able to use the bathroom when they need to and to get your attention when they're hurt. Kids can be really shy about these things. Make a point of addressing these issues at the first practice to let them know that it's okay to speak up when they need your help. Then make sure you listen and are aware when one of these issues arises. You should develop a tone of accessibility so that if kids are having any kind of problem in general, like with another player, they feel that they can come to you to discuss it.

CHAPTER 6

Sample Practices

Your first day of practice may make you feel like a kid again, especially if this is your first season. You're nervous about what to do, how to act, what the kids will think of you, and how they will respond. Relax. This chapter outlines in detail everything you need to do for several sample practices, beginning with the most basic and progressing through intermediate and more advanced practices. The basic practice is for all players. It introduces the fundamental skills of basketball, and all teams should work on the basics, both at the beginning and throughout the season. Players always benefit from practicing the fundamentals. Once you get going, you'll feel more comfortable about your coaching skills and the players' basketball skill levels, and you'll have everything under control. These sample practices are designed for use as a template for the rest of the season: they outline a basic structure of activities for your practices, with approximate time allotments and covering all aspects of the game. All of the drills listed in this chapter are described in greater detail in part 2, Drills: chapter 9 (Fundamental Drills), chapter 10 (Offensive Drills), or chapter 11 (Defensive Drills)—refer to the shadowed letter-number combination before the difficulty designation. As your team progresses in skills and experience, you can substitute some of the drills found in part 2 for those outlined in these practices.

Basic Beginning Practice
Team Meeting

This first team meeting should be to introduce yourself to the team, tell them what you expect from them, and learn their names (see Learn Their Names on page 51). Today you'll be learning or reviewing some of the fundamental skills of basketball, as well as introducing drills that you'll use throughout the season. The fundamental skills section of the practice will be a good opportunity for you to get to know your players and their abilities. Although all of the drills introduced in this basic practice are labeled as "easy" and are appropriate for beginners, they are just as important for the more advanced and older players. No matter how far a player gets in basketball, these basics are a key part of every practice.

Warm-Up

These warm-up exercises are a great way to start any practice, whether you are coaching complete novices or older kids with a lot of basketball experience. This series of jumps will help your players jump higher as the season gets going. You can first do them in sequence and then may wish to mix them up to keep the kids concentrating on your voice and instructions.

When doing quick jumps, players should always keep their hands above their shoulders.

- **Quick Jumps.** These are short, quick, stationary jumps. **F1** 👉

- **Power Jumps.** This warm-up drill helps your players develop stronger, more powerful jumps. **F2** 👉

- **Donkey Jumps.** The donkey jump is where your players jump up and kick their heels right up to their buttocks. **F3** 👉

- **Foot Fire.** This drill help players learn to get their feet moving. It is one of my all-time favorites, and I use it in all my camps with the kids. **F4** 👉

Fundamentals
Dribbling

Introduce dribbling with a demonstration and then review the five principles of a good dribble: finger-tip control, staying low, keeping your head up, being equally comfortable using either hand, and protecting the ball. Show these principles to players as you explain them. Bring out a chair and ask your players, "Can I do this in a chair?" Then sit in the chair and ask them to tell you what you are doing right—or wrong—with your dribble. Have a couple of players try dribbling in the chair, while the other players answer your questions about what they are doing right or wrong. Let the players know that one way to practice dribbling is to do it sitting in a chair—this will get them excited to try it at home and will let them know that they can be practicing their dribbling wherever they go—even on the bench.

- **Stationary Dribble.** This is the most basic drill to teach the fundamentals of dribbling. **F5** 👉

- **Heads-Up.** While dribbling, players have to call out the number of fingers you hold up, which teaches them to keep their heads up while concentrating on pushing the ball to the floor. **F6**

- **Crossover Move.** This drill gets players using both hands to dribble as they go from one hand to the other and back again. **F7**

- **Inside-Out Dribble.** Instead of placing their hands on the outside of the ball and pushing in (as in the crossover dribble), players place their hand on the inside of the ball and push out. As the kids get more comfortable with dribbling, they can learn to control the ball with this offensive move. **F7** →

Once your players are comfortable with stationary dribbling, it is time to get them moving with the following drills.

- **Moving Dribble.** This simple drill combines moving on cue with dribbling. **F8**

- **Dribble Tag.** Here is a game of tag that gets everyone moving and dribbling simultaneously. **F10**

- **Steal-the-Ball.** Players dribble while attempting to knock away their teammates' balls and protect their own. **F11**

The Steal-the-Ball drill teaches ball control. Players learn body and ball control while fending off their opponents' attempted steals.

Passing and Catching

These skills require hand-eye coordination and communication between players, as well as a good feel for the ball. Line your players up on the line, with every other person putting the ball behind her. Use a player or an assistant coach to demonstrate the proper techniques for a chest pass, bounce pass, and overhead pass, as well as the proper triple-threat position.

- **Partner Passing.** Players work with partners on their passing drills. Have them do a series of chest, bounce, and overhead passes, concentrating on turning their thumbs in and following through. **F16**

    The key to good catching is being ready to meet the pass: keeping knees bent and showing hands to the passer with palms up as a target for the passer. As the pass comes to the receiver, he jumps to catch it and restores his balance. The main components of catching are to have good balance, see the target, and meet the ball. The best way to learn this is to teach your players to concentrate, use their eyes, and work on the drills.

- **Soft Hands.** Players have to develop a touch and a feel for the ball, what is known as having *soft hands*. Developing soft hands entails catching the ball, bringing it in to the body, and getting in a balanced position to do the next motion. In this drill players must catch the ball with one hand. **F19**

Stopping and Pivoting

Pivoting helps players gain their balance after receiving a pass and is a good way to protect the ball from an opponent. There are proper ways to stop and establish a pivot foot. Demonstrate and explain the one-two stop and the two-footed stop, as well as the pivot.

- **Jump-Stop Left-Right and Right-Left.** This group drill introduces the one-two stop and pivoting. It can be done in either the whole gym or half of it. Players run, come to a one-two stop when you blow the whistle, and then pivot to various degrees. **F22**

- **Two-Footed Stop.** Players work on the two-footed stop and establishing a pivot foot. **F23**

- **Dribbling Whistle Pivot.** This drill incorporates dribbling with a jump stop and pivot. **F24**

Shooting

Players should really be encouraged to *drive to the basket*, which means to dribble the ball to the basket with speed and energy. When there's space available, and they can beat the person who is guarding them, your players should always be encouraged to drive.

The most important shot that players need to master is the layup. Players should start with the preferred hand. If they are on the right side of the basket, they push off on the left foot. They will drive with their right knee up in the air, put their hand behind the ball, and extend this hand. Baskets have squares behind them on the backboard. Players should lay the ball up in the back corner so the ball hits the square and goes through—it is important for the players to lay up the ball in the corner, not the center, of the square.

Driving the knee up in the air helps players to jump high, rather than long—if players are speed dribbling down the floor and take a layup without driving up the knee, they will keep going forward rather than up toward the basket. This is a problem area for most kids.

These drills introduce the basics of shooting. Shooting is discussed in detail in chapter 4.

- **Layup Rhythm.** This drill introduces the layup by slowing down the footwork so that players can get the rhythm of driving to the basket. **F28**

- **Two-Line Layup.** In this drill players are divided into two lines, one for shooting and one for rebounding. A player from the shooting line makes a layup while the player from the opposite line gets the rebound, passes to the next shooter, and joins the shooting line. This is a great drill to get everyone dribbling, shooting, rebounding, and passing. It's also a key warm-up drill for practices or games. **F31**

Defense

Call your players in and have them put their balls on the side of the court. These next drills are the basics of defense and don't require a ball. Explain the importance of defense to players and then explain and demonstrate the proper defensive stance (see Defensive Stance on page 43). By doing these drills you are developing a defensive philosophy. You are doing things with enthusiasm and are getting the players excited and focused on the skills they are learning. You're also teaching them to hustle, and you're setting a tone and atmosphere that defense is fun.

- **Stance.** Players assume the defensive stance and then hit the floor with their palms when the coach yells, "Stance!" The drill works on the defensive stance and is also a great warm-up drill. **D1**

- **Mirror.** This drill will teach your players to mirror the hand movements of their opponents. **D3**

- **Dick Harter.** Players assume the defensive position and slide their feet in the direction the coach indicates. The drill teaches the defensive slide, which is the way a player will move while staying right with his man. **D4** 👉

- **Zigzag.** Players move across the court in a zigzag pattern using the defensive slide. **D5** 👉

Offense

Faking a Shot or Pass

A *pass fake* is a pass not made, and a *shot fake* is a shot not taken. Whenever your players do these ball fakes, make sure that their knees stay down and that they move the ball so the defense can react. For a pass fake, for example, have them take a short step to the target and stay in a balanced position. They extend the ball with their hands up and then bring it in, ready to make a move when the defense reacts to that fake. If they are making a shot fake, they have their knees down and violently pump the ball up and forward, just a little bit over their head. This will cause the defense to come out of their balanced position as they try to block or contest the shot. When the defense does this, the player with the ball is now in a position to drive by them. When you're doing the two-player drills, have your players do a pass fake before they make the pass or a shot fake before they make the shot. The better fakers your players become, the more advantage they'll have on the court.

- **Dribble Jump-Stop Drill with Fake.** One player dribbles to the basket, does a jump stop, makes a shot fake, and then shoots. An opposing player rebounds. The same drill can incorporate a faked pass. **O1** 👉

Cutting

Cutting is simply learning how to move on the basketball court. As discussed in chapter 4, basketball is a sport played at angles. When your partner has the ball, you should take two steps to the ball and then go in a straight line to the basket, creating an angle on the cut. If you want to

Reading Your Partner

Whenever your players are doing a drill with two lines, and one line has to make a pass to the other line, try to get the players used to looking at each other. If they're thinking more about the drill than their partners, one player might be cutting, and the person with the ball hasn't even started dribbling toward the foul line to make the pass. Or the person at the foul line has already started dribbling in, and the person who's supposed to receive the pass is looking at the ceiling, not at the passer. When your players get into the habit of looking at each other, they will get comfortable varying their pace and making their cuts.

Key to Success: Be Flexible

You may find that it is difficult to fit in everything outlined for this basic practice in one session because you have to spend time teaching the fundamentals and drills. It depends on whether you are coaching beginners or more experienced players, and on the mix of skills within the team. Use this basic practice for as many sessions as necessary, gradually adding new concepts and drills as your players are ready. If things take longer than expected, skip an area and pick it up another time. Conversely, if you're moving right along, spend more time on the competitive areas such as the Fast Break Drill and Combination Transition Drill. The kids will enjoy these drills, and you will be using them and building on them often throughout the season. Remember that you won't get everything perfect in the first few practices—or maybe even throughout the entire season. The point is to keep it fun for everyone while learning some solid basics.

receive a pass, you should take two steps to the basket and then come back at an angle to free yourself. Playing the game at angles—learning to move strategically—is crucial.

- **Back-Cut to Layup.** This is a good basic drill. One player heads toward a teammate with the ball, cuts to the basket, receives a pass, and shoots. **03** 🏀

- **Give-and-Go.** As the name suggests, a player passes to a teammate, cuts toward the basket, and receives the ball again for a layup. This drill reinforces the principle of moving at angles and taking two steps away from where we want to go before going there. **06** 🏀

- **Fast Break.** Players are divided into three lines, one with the ball under the basket and one to either side. The player with the ball dribbles out to the foul line and passes to one of the two players running wide down the court. This drill introduces the concept of a fast break and sprinting down the floor. **09** 🏀

Ending Activity
- **Shooting Competition.** This fun game is competitive, challenging, and a great way to end practice. **F36** 🏀

Wrap-Up/Doggy Bag
Bring your players into the huddle and tell them they did a great job. Give them something to work on for the next session—practicing their dribbling might be a good one for this first practice. Explain that this first practice may have moved a little slower because you had to teach a lot of the drills, and that the next practice will be much quicker because you'll be doing a lot of the same things. End with a team cheer, "One, two, three, team!" and then announce the day and time of the next practice.

Intermediate Practice

Team Meeting

Today when you meet with your players, tell them the emphasis is on sprinting down the floor: on offense, if you don't have the ball, you sprint down the floor. On defense, as soon as you lose possession, you sprint the other way.

Warm-Up

You should know everyone's name by now, so make a game of it. Point around the floor and name all of your players, and then tell your players on the whistle to give you two claps for managing to memorize all of their names.

- **Jumping.** Begin with Quick Jumps **F1**, Power Jumps **F2**, and Donkey Jumps **F3**. 👉

- **Foot Fire.** Have your players concentrate on light, quick movements. **F4** 👉

- **Stance** **D1** 👉

Fundamentals
Dribbling

- **Stationary Dribble.** Work on stationary dribbling with both the right and left hands, concentrating on the five dribbling fundamentals. **F5** 👉

The next step in the dribbling progression is for players to learn to change speed and direction, and to incorporate offensive moves in their dribbling.

- **Stop-and-Go.** Players dribble down a line of cones, stopping and then accelerating at each cone. This is a good drill to practice changing speed and direction while dribbling. **F13** 👉

Above Right: Donkey Jumps drill.

Right: The Stop-and-Go drill requires players to change speed and direction while dribbling.

- **Stop-and-Cross.** This drill introduces offensive dribbling moves by combining an abrupt stop with a crossover move. **F15**

- **Steal-the-Ball.** Repeat the drill from the beginning practice, with one change. Whenever a player's ball goes out of bounds, she has to stand outside the lines and work on her stationary dribbling while the others finish the game. **F11**

Passing

- **Partner Passing F16 , Dribble Passing F17 , and Pass-Receive F18 .** →

Catching

- **Anticipating the Pass.** Here the receiver has his back turned to the passer until the pass is thrown. This drill helps players to concentrate and react immediately to a ball on its way. **F20**

Pivoting

- **Dribble, Jump-Stop, Pivot, Pass.** This is a great drill that combines all of the fundamental skills that you've worked on so far in this practice. Even highly skilled players should be doing this one. **F25**

Shooting

- **Pull-Up.** Here players stop short of a normal layup and make a shot. The drill teaches your players to pull up before shooting, which they'll need to do when the other team's defense is waiting by the basket. **F30**

Rebounding

All of the jumping drills that you've worked on are important in rebounding and will help your players to become better rebounders. Make sure that they know the best way to get a rebound is at its highest peak. On the defensive end, it is also important that you stress the idea that each player should locate her man when a shot is taken to prevent this player from getting an offensive rebound. Each player should know to make contact with her man and to box or block out this opponent. The keys to offensive rebounding involve reading the "bounce" of a missed shot and staying aggressive.

- **Mirror F39**

- **Toss off the Backboard.** In this drill the coach bounces the ball off the backboard, and players line up to make rebounds. This is a good drill to teach young players to actually get up and receive the ball at its highest peak. **F40**

- **One-on-One Toss off the Backboard.** This variation adds a competitive element to the Toss off the Backboard. **F41**

- **Two-on-Two Toss off the Backboard** **F42**

Defense

- **Mirror** **D3**

- **One-on-One Full-Court.** Players are paired off, and the drill begins with the player with the ball getting by his defender. After that it is a one-on-one contest ending in a basket or a turnover. The drill stresses that a player on defense should never be beaten by an offensive player—no matter what, the defense should run to catch up. **D8**

Offense

- **Ball Fake Game.** This game teaches *convincing* ball fakes. Players find that it is fun to fake out a teammate. **O2**

- **Fast Break** **O9**

- **Fast Break Rebound and Outlet.** In this drill your players will learn to rebound a ball, *outlet* it (pass it to a teammate to start a fast break), and run hard down the side of the floor to receive a return pass. Communication is vital for a successful fast break, and by yelling, "Ball," and "Outlet," your players will become accustomed to talking the play through to each other. **O11**

- **Give-and-Go** **O6**

- **Combination Transition.** This drill is one that you'll incorporate into most of your practices throughout the season. Your players will also really like it because it simulates a game situation—it is fun, fast, and competitive. The skills they learn in this drill include offensive and defensive transition, fast break, and give-and-go. The drill is essentially a two-on-one going down the court one way and a two-on-two coming back. During the two-on-one, offensive players learn to pass to the open player and to dribble the ball up court quickly. During the two-on-two, they are definitely playing in twos, and the concepts of two-player basketball, particularly the pick and roll, should be encouraged. The point is to give your players a feel for playing in twos, working on both offensive and defensive transitions, and working on playing together as a team. Later you will build this drill into a three-on-three and four-on-four. **O12** 👉

- **Pass and Screen Away.** This drill is designed to free a teammate without the ball so that she will become open to receive a pass. In this play, Player A passes the ball and then moves to free her teammate by becoming a screen (getting between her teammate and the defender). **07** 👉

- **Three-on-Three Games.** Divide your players into teams and let them play three-on-three games. They will need to learn to move on the court and solve their own problems. Start their minigames from a formation of a point and two wings. Have them play for two or three baskets, each time starting from this formation, and then rotate your teams. Three-on-three games incorporate give-and-go, pass and screen on the ball, and pass and screen away from the ball, and the games pull together some of the skills the players have learned in other drills. In terms of skill level, this activity is for all levels. Players get out of it what they've learned to date; they play the three-on-three at the level they're at and get a feel for what it's like to have more than one or two players on the court. 👉 → 👉 → 👉

In the Pass and Screen Away drill, one player positions himself to block, or screen, a defender, thus freeing a teammate to receive a pass.

Ending Activity

- **Dribble Shoot Relay.** This game is competitive and incorporates dribbling, shooting, and rebounding. **F38** 👉

Wrap-Up/Doggy Bag

Bring your players in and tell them what a good job they've done. Announce what skill they should work on until the next practice, depending on what didn't go as well as you'd hoped. Remind them when the next practice is and then do a team cheer.

Advanced Intermediate Practice 1
Team Meeting

When you meet your players at this practice, tell them that today you'll be emphasizing passing to an open person: if somebody is more open than you are, pass them the ball. You'll also continue to concentrate on sprinting down the floor and defense.

Warm-Up

- **Two-Line Layup** **F31**
- **Quick Jumps** **F1** , **Power Jumps** **F2** , and **Donkey Jumps** **F3**
- **Quick Hands/Quick Feet** **D2**
- **Foot Fire** **F4**
- **Stance** **D1**

Fundamentals
Dribbling

- **Stationary Dribble** **F5**
- **Crossover Move** **F7** →
- **Full-Court Stop and Dribble.** Players are required to change speed, hands, and direction while dribbling upon whistle cues **F14**

Passing

- **Pass-Receive.** Here players form two facing lines. The player at the head of one line passes to the head of the opposite line, and then the two players run to the end of the opposite lines. The coach calls out various passes, and players must respond. This is a great warm-up drill that gets the kids moving, listening, and working on passing and catching. **F18**

Catching

- **Bad Pass.** This drill teaches players to react to difficult passes. **F21**

Pivoting

- **Combination.** In this drill a player dribbles out, makes a jump stop facing *away* from the receiver, pivots, and then passes. It combines many fundamental skills. **F26**

Shooting

- **Crossover Layup.** This combines a standard layup drill with a crossover move to emphasize movement on the court. **F32**

- **Layup Strength.** In this strength-building exercise, players shoot layups against a backboard or wall, catching the ball and shooting again repeatedly. **F29**

- **Combination Layup.** This drill combines many fundamental skills, with the emphasis on the layup. **F33**

Rebounding

- **Mirror** **F39**

- **One-on-One Toss off the Backboard** **F41**

Defense

- **Three-Player Combination Transition.** This is the same combination transition drill from earlier practices, where your players work on defensive skills in a game-simulated situation. This time you will play three players on a side. **O13**

- **Two-on-Two Shell.** Two defensive players guard two offensive players in the wings while the coach makes passes to the offensive players from center court and they return the passes. With this drill your players work on the concepts of playing the opponent in relationship to where the ball is and going from ball side to help side as necessary. **D12**

- **Two-on-Two Defensive Transition.** Two offensive players face off against two defensive players at one end of the court, with two additional players placed at the opposite end of the court. As soon as the offensive players score or turn over the ball, they have to sprint the length of the court to guard the two waiting players. The point of this drill is to get your players instinctively turning from offense to defense. Instead of walking around and just changing lines when the ball is turned over, they learn to sprint the floor, find and call out their particular man, and take up a defensive position. **D20**

- **Four-on-Four-on-Four Competition.** This is a defensive game, where a stop (without fouling) equals a score. Don't count baskets—count stops to develop the players' pride in the defense. **D18**

Offense

- **Fast Break Drill with Layup.** Here the fast break drill finishes with a layup. **O10**

- **Pick and Roll.** Pick and roll employs screening to free a player with the

In a pick and roll, one player jumps in to screen a teammate with the ball, who then comes off the screen shoulder to shoulder with the blocking teammate and who either drives to the basket or passes to an open player. Here the coach demonstrates.

ball so that he can either drive to the basket for a layup or pass to another open player. **O8**

- **Free Throw Shooting** **F37**

- **Intermediate Out-of-Bounds Play.** This is a set box play designed to bring the ball from out-of-bounds down the court to the basket. It uses a diagonal pick and roll, and it has a lot of deception with some good screening angles so that the young players can be successful. **O16**

- **Shooting Progression.** Players shoot from various spots on the court, incorporating fakes. **F35**

- **Down and Back.** This is a five-on-five scrimmage where every shot made, whether or not it results in a basket, is a transition. After three transitions, play stops for evaluation and line changes. **O17**

- **Shooting.** Because the above drill is fatiguing, follow it with a round of five foul shots to recuperate. Emphasize good shooting technique and rebounding position.

Ending Activity

- **Shooting Competition.** Use both baskets, and keep score. **F36**

Wrap-Up/Doggy Bag

Free Throw/Foul Shot: Keep It Consistent

A simple routine with good shooting mechanics is the key to good free throw shooting. Have players do the same thing every time: if one player is comfortable when she bounces the ball three times, takes a deep breath, and then shoots, have her do that all the time. Another player might be more comfortable taking only one dribble. The key is to always keep the same routine. Because the shooter has time during a free throw, he should place his hands behind the ball in the same place every time. Most shooters like the feel of their hands going across the seams. Encourage your young players to find the air hole of the ball and to place their index finger across the seam below the air hole. This gives them a consistent landmark for hand placement every time. During practice sessions I like the concept of half the team members practicing free throws at one end with an assistant while the other members work on offensive and defensive drills at the other end with the head coach. The groups then rotate after five-minute segments.

Advanced Intermediate Practice 2

Team Meeting

Today when you meet with your players, tell them that the emphasis of this practice is on talking while on defense—players should concentrate on calling, "Ball!" and on yelling, "Shot!" when someone shoots and yells, "Help!" as they learn the help position.

Warm-Up

- **Quick Hands/Quick Feet** **D2**

- **Foot Fire** **F4**

- **Stance** **D1**

- **Mirror** **D3**

Fundamentals

Dribbling

- **Stationary Dribble.** Players use both right and left hands, shifting when you blow your whistle. **F5**

- **Stop-and-Go and Stop-and-Cross.** Set up cones across the court. Combine these two drills to get the players changing speed and direction while dribbling, as well as incorporating an offensive move. Everyone should go through the drill five times, moving all the time. **F13** **F15**

Passing/Catching/Shooting

- **Two-Line Layup Back-Cut.** Players are divided into two lines. Those with the ball dribble up to the elbow; players in the other line do a back-cut, receive a bounce pass, and shoot. **F34**

- **Quick Reversal.** Three players advance down the court making quick passes and finishing with a shot and rebound. The object of this drill is to move the zone with quick passes. **O18**

Rebounding
- **One-on-One Toss off the Backboard** **F41**

- **Two-on-Two Toss off the Backboard.** This is the same drill as above except that another pair of offensive/defensive players are added on the other side. Have the defensive players be in the deny position, and when the coach shoots, have them play live, with no restrictions, no stopping for drills, etc.—a real "game" situation. **F42**

Defense

- **Combination Transition.** Start with a two-player combination transition drill and move up to a three-player combination transition drill. **D17**

- **Three-on-Three Stop Game.** Players play a three-on-three offensive/defensive game where the only way they can score is by a defensive stop. Start the game by passing with a screen away—after that the players can do anything they want. Emphasize that if the person isn't open, they need to remember to back-cut and be aware that the defense will really be trying to stop them. Play this game to four stops. The losers will do one sprint down to the end of the court and back. **D16**

- **Intermediate Out-of-Bounds Play.** This time, rather than starting with a skeleton out-of-bounds play, go directly to playing against defense. Have two teams, each with three chances to score. **O16**

- **Beating the Press.** This drill is designed to harass the offensive and make them really work to move the ball upcourt. In this drill five offensive players are assigned: one player brings the ball in from out-of-bounds and passes to one of two teammates trying to free themselves near the foul line; two other teammates are positioned at half-court. The defense should be very active in denying their man and possessing the ball. **O20**

- **Three-on-Three Defensive Transition.** In this drill your players will be working on both offense and defense in a three-on-three formation. **D21**

Offense

- **Zone Offense.** There are two basic concepts to a zone offense: forming an offensive triangle and moving the ball quickly. In a zone offense, ball movement is more critical than player movement. This drill helps players create a good zone offense **O19**

- **Five-on-Five Scrimmage.** In this drill, players play in a gamelike situation for 2 minutes, receive feedback from you about things they need to improve, and then play for another 2-minute block. **O21**

- **Free Throw Shooting.** This drill emphasizes good shooting technique and rebounding position. **F37**

Ending Activity

- **Dribble Tag** **F10** 👉

Wrap-Up

End the practice with a team cheer.

Questions and Answers

Q. In the first practice we didn't get through even half of the recommended drills and practice segments of the basic practice. What should I focus on if I can't get through the whole thing?

A. The first day of the season or the first time that you do a drill you are bound to spend a lot of time teaching it. Once your team knows the drill, the next time it will go twice as fast. So the next practice you should start right at the beginning, go through the same drills and you'll see that they get through them a lot quicker. Keep the routine the same for every practice: do the same drills over and over, and you'll start getting through all your recommended segments as the players learn the drills within a few practices. Beginning players may work within the basic beginning practice for the entire season, depending on the ages and abilities of your particular group. Kids who have played the game for a couple of years might be ready for the intermediate practice but may use those drills for the entire season. The most important thing is to stay within the abilities of your team members.

Q. I have had the good luck to get a group of kids that seem to really pick up the skills quickly. We have had two practices, and I have found that the kids are going through the blocks more quickly than the time I've allotted. They are getting bored, and I'm left with a big chunk of time at the end with nothing to do. How should I address this?

A. If you have a good group of kids, and they're all making their layups, for example, and they get bored with just the layup drill, make the drill a competitive game. They have to make ten in a row on the right side and call out the numbers. Even the talented, experienced player will feel the tension building as the layups start getting counted off. You can do the same thing with the dribble series, dribbling up to the cones, by putting a time allotment on it or seeing how fast they can complete the drill while still maintaining proper form. Do more relay races where they have to make a move or a basket. Do more competitive shooting where they count the baskets. Anytime you see interest waning you should turn the drill into some type of fun competition. You can also add more drills to each practice from the skill-building section, combine two practices in one, or let the kids scrimmage more—but remember to keep it fun.

Q. We've had three practices, and while the kids are enjoying themselves, they just aren't getting the skills. I've been trying to build on what we've done from the previous practice, but I feel like I have to keep reteaching the basics each time. Do I keep trying to move on, or just start all over again?

A. It's going to take time. If they're having fun, that's what really matters. Don't hesitate to keep to the basics as long as necessary. Basketball can be a very, very difficult game to learn, never mind to master, and the increments and the improvements your players show may be slight each session in regard to skills and drills. Don't kid yourself that after two or three practices the kids are going to be Larry Birds or Michael Jordans—it's just not going to happen. What you are giving them is the ability to progress and improve at a slow rate but with a foundation that will help them really improve and take a big step from one year to the next. Don't expect miracles, and you won't be disappointed. Be patient.

Q. I have a player with great skills who zips passes to her teammates that they can't handle. How should I handle this?

A. You need to impress upon the player that the only good pass is one that can be caught by her teammates. Zipping passes that can't be handled is often a way in which better players differentiate themselves from their teammates in terms of their ability. This must be addressed verbally. Suggest, then, as an alternative to the pass that can't be handled, either a softer chest pass or most preferably a bounce pass. The bounce pass is the most effective pass in the game because of the difficulty in stealing it, but it also is easier to handle because it reaches the recipient at a slower speed.

Q. Some of my players are ready for advanced moves, like pick and roll and help-side defense, and others can hardly dribble. Should I get an assistant and divide the team into ability groups for practice?

A. All teams are going to have players with a large variance from top to bottom in ability. The important element is that all players improve, are challenged, and have fun. Again, when competing one-on-one and two-on-two, have the stronger players play against one another. Continue to do basic drills together, stressing fundamentals to lower levels and challenging the stronger players to make their moves more precise.

Q. My team is ready for more complicated skill drills. We've already mastered the ones in the book. What do I do now?

A. Drills are never mastered. For example, consider the crossover move. The crossover dribble is when a player dribbles down, comes to a stop, fakes one way, puts a hand on the outside of the ball and then pushes it across the body, picks it up with the opposite hand, and starts dribbling again in a straight line. A player may be able to complete the drill, but the lower and quicker that crossover can work, the better the player will fake. A player can always take a longer step or can lean or really get comfortable; he can get in a rhythm and get that crossover so hard and low, and so hard and quick, that no one could ever intercept it. I don't think you'll ever have a player who can do all the skills with his nonpreferred hand as well as with his preferred hand. So anytime someone thinks, "Well, I can do that. What else should I do?" he should go right to his weak hand and make sure he is doing all the drills with both hands.

You can also combine different drills to make them more difficult. The possibilities are endless. It might be a great doggy bag to challenge your players with a drill variation that keeps their interest levels high.

CHAPTER 7

The Game

Rules to Live By

No matter how many years you have participated in sports, you'll never lose that butterflies-in-your-stomach feeling before the first game of the season. This is the first test of how well all of your team's hard work will pay off, and you may consider the first game as a test of your coaching ability, as well. It will be easy to get caught up in the excitement of scoring against opponents, and it will be tempting to judge the success or failure of your team— and your coaching skill—by the final score. Remember, though, that one team will win this game, and one will lose, and you should be prepared to accept either outcome with grace and good humor. Either way, your team will have the opportunity to display the skills you've worked on, and you will all learn your strengths and weaknesses on the court.

Set an Example

The most important role you'll play in the game will be as an example to your players. You will need to prepare yourself, to visualize your behavior and actions during the game, to control your anxiety and excitement. No matter how much you talk to your players about good sportsmanship and the importance of respecting authority, your actions are going to speak much more forcefully about what you really believe than will your words.

Respect the Officials

Meet the officials before the game, whether they're paid professionals, volunteer parents, or high school kids, shake their hands, and show them the respect they deserve. During the game, if they make a mistake, forget about it and concentrate on being positive and getting your team to do the things that you've worked on in practice. If an official makes a bad call against your team, right away, as soon as the call is made, give your players something to do so that they don't have the time to even think about what might

When Your Players Misbehave

If you see players that give a physical sign—stomp up and down, throw the ball—after an official's call, you have to discipline them. Take them out of the game, sit them on the bench, and tell them that behavior is unacceptable. Let them know that they are a part of a classy team, and that they are expected to act with class and to treat others with respect. You shouldn't berate your player or belittle her, and it doesn't need to be a public scolding, but you definitely need to give that player a clear and immediate message that her behavior will not be tolerated. Ever.

have been a bad call. Tell them to sprint back and concentrate on defense; ask them, "Where's your man?" All too often coaches and parents will spend time talking to the officials or making some comment, and the kids pick up on that. At no time should you really question an official's call.

Officials are going to make mistakes. It's not so much the mistake they make that's important, but it's how you as a coach, and you as a team, react to it. If you let those mistakes upset you, it's going to adversely affect the way your team plays. If you just forget it and concentrate on the things that you can control, it's a nice, positive habit to get into. You should also tell your team that no one is allowed to question an official's call—and be prepared to stick by that.

It's important that as soon as the game is over, no matter what the score or how bad you think the officiating was, you go right up to the officials, shake their hands, and thank them. Most of the time the officials at your games are volunteers, or they aren't being paid very much, and they always deserve your thanks and respect.

Be Ready

Just as you need to be prepared before every practice, you will need to have a game plan established well before game time rolls around. Your game plan will include who will start the game, positions, substitutions and rotations, playing time, and so on. You should decide beforehand what you will do if you are winning by a lot, barely winning, barely losing, or losing by quite a lot. If anything, you will need to be more organized and prepared than ever, since your players will be nervous and excited and will look to your example to guide their behavior. When they get to the gym, get them organized immediately and out on the court, working on some of the drills you've used in practice.

Use the following drill sequence as a possible game warm-up template. These drills will get your players loosened up.

1. **Layup drill:** both sides

2. **Back-cut drill:** both sides

Why Bring Balls to a Game?

Many times when teams are warming up for a game, there aren't enough balls available to them. If you have one or two balls for your whole team and you're all trying to warm up, there will be two kids shooting and twelve kids underneath the basket fighting for the rebound. Some of the little guys never come up with it and never get a turn to shoot. Try to get at least one ball for every two people, if not one per player. It will give your warm-up some structure and will ensure that everybody is getting enough shots at the basket for warm-up. During the game make sure that these balls are put away so the kids on the bench are not tempted to play with them.

3. **Two-line shooting drill:** both sides

4. **Partner free shooting drill:** two lines, with half rebounding and half shooting. Always pair up your players so that your entire team isn't swarming under the basket, fighting over balls. Switch positions after making a shot or after a minute.

Inbounding the Ball from the Sidelines.

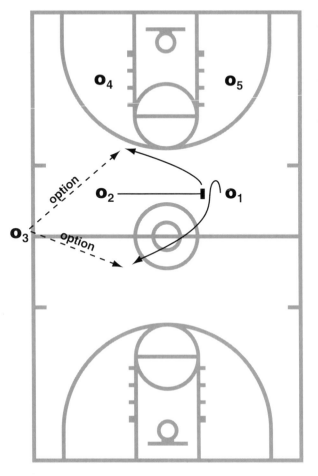

Getting Going

Action on the court will be fast paced and exciting, but you may find you're not quite sure how to get it started. Here are some guidelines for getting the ball in play.

Opening Tip-off

The player who jumps—most likely the center or the one who jumps the highest—faces the basket that the team warmed up at. The basic formation for the tip-off is to have the two forwards on the sides of the circle, the point guard in back of the person jumping, and the other guard in front of the person jumping. The point guard acts as a safety in case the other team wins the tip-off. If the ball is tipped forward to the other guard, the two forwards are in position to run the floor and may be able to get an easy layup.

Inbounding the Ball

From the Sidelines. During the game, the ball will inevitably go out of bounds over the sidelines. Your team will now have to make an inbounds play to get the game going again (see diagram at left). The referee will hand the ball to one of your players (you should designate the player who will always take the ball out, generally your best passer). That player may not move from the designated spot to pass it in. She has five seconds to pass the ball to a teammate. Because some teams will try to deny the inbounds pass, teams should set up a designated play to get the ball in.

The basic inbounds play, whether it's on the sidelines or under the offensive goal, is a box formation with the guards set up in the back of the box and the bigger players in the front of the box. Have a forward take the ball out (usually the 3 or small forward). The players in front of the box should set a screen for the guard on the same side of the box. Usually during a sideline out of bounds, the point guard will receive the ball to get the team into an offensive set. During inbounds under the offensive goal, the players coming off the screen to receive the ball can vary. Also, there are ways to switch who screens for whom. For instance, instead of the two players in the front of the box screening for the ones in the back of the box, have the players on the right side of the box screen for the players on the left side of the box.

From the End Line. The same formation for inbounding the ball from the sideline should be used when taking the ball out along the end line (see diagram at right). If the other team scores a basket, your team is now allowed to run the end line to help pass in the ball. There is no designated spot from which the player taking the ball in must pass.

Against Full-Court Pressure. Inbounding the ball against full-court pressure requires the effective use of space. In most of the out-of-bounds plays already discussed, the small forward or the 3 will take it out. The same is true for an inbounds play going against pressure. The two guards should line up on their defensive foul line facing the ball, in a tandem fairly close together. The bigger players (the 4 and 5) should line up at half court, where one is on one sideline and the other is on the other sideline. Have the front guard break to the left and the back guard break to the right. Have the 5 man take two steps to the ball and then cut to the hoop. Have the 4 man take two steps away from the ball, then cut to the ball. Most of the time, the ball should be inbounded to one of the guards, preferably the point guard. Once a guard receives the ball, all the other players should be instructed to "clear out" and give space so the guard can bring the ball up. If there is a problem with getting the ball in

Inbounding the Ball from the Defensive End Line.

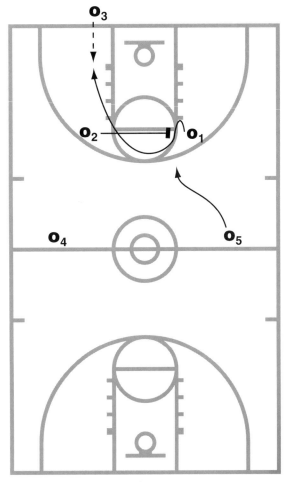

bounds, then have the two guards set a screen for each other instead of just breaking away. If it is a trapping defense, one man will always be open. The players should be instructed to pass the ball to the open man if they are trapped or double teamed. If the defense is playing a zone defense, then use the same concepts to inbound the ball, then instead of clearing out for the ball to be brought up court with the dribble, have the players pass the ball to bring it up.

Explain Your Substitution Pattern

This is a huge issue, with ramifications well beyond simply who's out on the court at a given time. When you bring your players together before the start of the game, explain to them the substitution pattern—who will go in, who will come out, and when. You should begin thinking about this well before the first game, and probably you will have begun this discussion with the players at the last practice or two (they will ask you about it, whether you bring it up or not). Every player on the team will have a number or a letter. If you have 12 players on your team, you will start Players 1, 2, 3, 4, and 5. On the full substitution, which you should do midway through the first quarter (usually after 4 minutes of the 8-minute quarter) you will substitute in players 6, 7, 8, 9, and 10. The next full substitution will happen at the end of the first quarter and will be Players 11, 12, 1, 2, and 3. You do need to figure out how many ball handlers you have and relate the rotation and numbers to them. Don't just line up the kids in random order. Plan it ahead of time and look at how the combinations will come out as the game progresses. Put your kids in an order that will work well. Otherwise you might end up with a group that cannot bring the ball down the floor or that is just going to flounder.

By doing this numerical substitution you guarantee your players equal playing time, and you take the question of ability out of the game entirely, in regard to who gets to play more than anyone else. This is the fairest way to reward all of your players—if they come to practice and play with enthusiasm, they play in the games.

If possible, meet the other coach before the game, not only to establish a friendly atmosphere but also to discuss how he or she will handle substitution. The ideal situation is that your league will have a policy that everybody plays an equal amount. That may or may not be the case.

Ideally, you'll have ten people so that everybody will play half the game. If you have many more players than that, talk to the other coach and consider playing longer quarters: instead of playing 8-minute quarters, try to play 10-minute quarters, so that all the players have a chance to play longer.

Remind all the players how to enter the game as a sub—they are to report to the scorer that they are going in, and they must remain at the scorer's table waiting for a whistle.

Time-Outs: Stick to the Basics When Things Aren't Going Well

Make sure that whenever there's a time-out everyone runs to the bench. You want your team to sprint on and off the court every time, whatever the situation. Tell your players that everything they do in a game should be done the same way they do it at practice—move with energy and enthusiasm.

Make sure everyone is in a circle to keep all players involved, and stick to the basics. If there's a situation where things aren't going right, just try to make the game seem shorter. Say, "Hey, for the next 4 minutes, let's make sure we out-rebound this team," or "For the next 4 minutes, everyone should sprint back so that they don't get any layups." It's important sometimes that they concentrate on other things than the score, particularly if things aren't going well. You can call a time-out and stick to the basics, even if you're way behind. Too often coaches get wrapped up in telling their players to run specific plays instead of saying, "Hey, if you're open, shoot the ball."

Players will learn so much if you can get them to run into the huddle and to run out of the huddle. If the referee calls a foul and there's a foul shot, get them to run to the foul line. Just keep them moving aggressively and working hard. Keep your goals small and immediate, and make sure you stay positive: if you get negative, then your players will get negative. If you lead by example and are cheering and getting your team sprinting, it will be a rewarding experience. You can tell a joke to ease the tension or point out all the excited spectators who are there just to cheer them on. Ask them, "Isn't this a blast?"

Manage the Clock

Most of the offensive problems with youth basketball are that they commit a *turnover*, meaning a change in possession due to a bad pass or someone stealing the ball from the dribbler before a shot is taken. To me, it is more important to get a shot off quickly, and I feel teams shouldn't be trying to run delay offenses to manage the clock. It is an extremely difficult concept to teach and shouldn't be an emphasis.

As a general rule you want to preserve time-outs for the end of the game, in case you need to set up last-minute schemes. However, do not become overly concerned with this point. Use time-outs to teach and to steer your team back on track when they are clearly veering off.

When the game is nearing completion and your team is winning, and if your players can handle the ball with some proficiency, try to have them pass the ball and avoid shooting until a good shot develops. If you are losing and the game is nearing completion, do not panic and make risky decisions, but encourage your players to run up and down the court, to move the ball quickly from the defensive end to the offensive end, and to work quickly to develop a shot. Full-court defensive pressure, if you have taught it, is the optimal way to catch up when you are losing.

What about Stats?

It is fine to use statistics (points scored, rebounds, shots taken) at halftime to make points. Obviously, if there are numerous turnovers, you want to make sure your better ball handlers handle the ball. If your team is getting grossly out-rebounded, you could emphasize boxing out.

Always use the stats to challenge and encourage, never to discourage. "We turned the ball over only five times in the first half. This is a result of our hard work in practice on ball handling! Let's see if we can keep it to four turnovers in the second half." Or, "We allowed 12 offensive rebounds in the first half, which led to at least 20 easy points for the other team. You are all clearly working hard to go after the rebounds, but each of you needs to find your man and box him out before looking at the shot. . . just like we worked on in practice. Let's hold them to under 6 offensive rebounds in the second half." It's important to rarely use any one player's individual stats either to expose weakness or to bring praise. The latter is more common, but it brings the wrong message of putting the individual ahead of the team and runs the risk of the player becoming too concerned with his own statistics. Instead, point out individual good hustling or good shooting.

Whether you use stats or not, the main emphasis should be on the areas you can control. Is the team sprinting back on defense? Does each player know whom she is guarding? Is the team fast breaking? Should we do more screening in the offense? What you should stress at halftime are the main concepts used and what can be improved upon.

End the Game Positively

As soon as the game ends, bring your team in and acknowledge some of the positive things they did—how they encouraged each other, how they hustled, how they stayed in their defensive stance. Don't concentrate on the score, whether you lost *or won*. Mention that the team will need to work on some things, but that you'll take care of those in practice. Then give yourselves a cheer, such as "One, two, three, team!" or "One, two, three, together!"

Then the next thing to do is to respect your opponents, and that's something that you should really reinforce to your players. No matter what the score is in the game, make sure that you always respect your opponents. Give them a cheer such as, "Two, four, six, eight, who do we appreciate?" and name the team that you played. After that, your whole team—including you—should get in a line and shake hands with the other team. You should also go up and thank the coach and the referees. It's an important part of setting an example of good sportsmanship and what athletics should be about.

Encourage your players to approach games with enthusiasm and sportsmanship.

Taking Stock after the Game

After each game is a good time to assess where you are and where you want to progress. It can be tempting to focus entirely on how many points are scored or how many games are won as indicators of how the team is doing—if they are winning games, the season is going great; if they are losing, the season is going poorly. Rather than allowing game scores to dictate your sense of how your season is shaping up, remember that the whole point of coaching your players is to help them become better basketball players, individually and as a team.

Games will reveal your team's strengths, as well as its most glaring weaknesses. Use games as vehicles for evaluating progress in skill development and in how well the players are coming together as a team. The first question you should ask yourself is, "Are the players improving individually?" Make a checklist of the different skill areas and assess how your players are progressing in developing these skills. Some of these areas could include

- Dribbling better with both hands
- Getting better with layups
- Running the floor hard
- Picking up the defense
- Communicating to each other on the court
- Playing with energy and enthusiasm
- Supporting each other on and off the court

Then look at the team and try to assess the team's overall performance in terms of generalities: in what areas do they excel, and where do they have problems? Congratulate yourself and your team members on the aspects of the game that they do well—it is due in large part to your help that they have accomplished these team skills. When you can pinpoint

What Defines Success?

Success is getting a team to play hard, play together, and reach its potential while having fun. Each kid needs to enjoy his experience being on a basketball team. There is no substitute for enthusiasm, encouragement, and personal attention from the coach. A major component of this fun is derived from each kid gaining a sense of contribution to the team. Find each kid's niche and let her know that she is doing a good job. If a natural niche doesn't develop, be creative to find a way in which that kid can thrive, experience success, and gain a sense of contributing to the team. Finally, stress improvement and development. Applaud the areas in which you notice improvement in individuals and in the team as a whole, and point out in a positive manner areas in which players and the team can improve. Present a challenge and set goals. Winning games is an obvious and healthy objective, but make it clear at least once per season that your team played well despite losing and explain that it is *how* the team strives to win that is important. Never miss an opportunity to encourage, challenge, and have fun.

problems your team has during games, take the problem apart piece by piece and see how you can address it.

Here are several common problems that young teams have and some ways to address them.

Problem: The Other Team Is Stealing Your Team's Passes

There's a good chance that if the other team is winning, it is because they get layups after stealing the ball. They may be *stealing the pass*. That means that your team is dribbling the ball down the floor and might try to run a pass and screen away, or a give-and-go, or a pass and cut, but the defense is anticipating the pass and intercepting it.

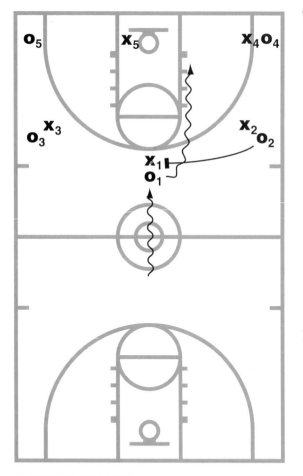

Wing Sets Screen. When one of the wings sets a screen on the ball, the dribbler is free to drive to the basket.

Solution:

1. Drive to the basket.

The first thing you should look at is how wide your team is playing in the wings. If they are playing wide, there is a lot of space there for the person with the ball to try to dribble by his opponent. Encourage your player with the ball to drive to the basket. If your players aren't skilled enough to beat their defenders, have one of the wings set a screen on the ball as soon as the dribbler comes over the half-court line (see diagram at left). By freeing the dribbler this way, your players won't have to make a lot of passes before they get an opportunity to score. They'll use the space the defense is giving them by trying to steal the passes to drive to the basket (see page 37).

2. Cut to the basket.

A second way for players to avoid having their passes stolen is to keep cutting to the basket on their own side of the floor (see page 85). If Player 2 is on the right wing and Player 4 is in the right corner, and if the dribbler, Player 1, comes over the half-court line, Player 2 knows that her defender will try to steal the ball. Player 2 should cut to the basket. Player 4 will see Player 2 cutting to the basket and will replace Player 2 on the wing. When Player 4 comes up from the corner, she'll be open for the pass. Now the dribbler can pass to Player 4 and then go screen away or go screen for Player 4 on the ball. If Player 4's man is trying to steal the ball or deny her the ball, she could cut to the basket, and

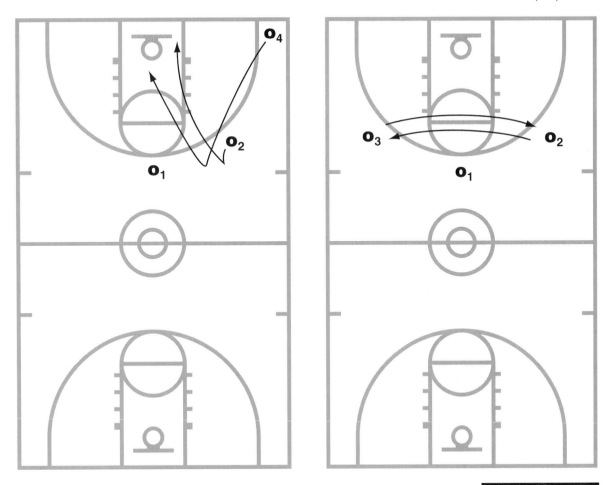

Player 2 would come back and replace her. It's important to create this movement when teams are stealing the pass (see pages 37 and 114).

(see pages 37 and 114)

3. Exchange wings.

Another solution to pass stealing is to *exchange wings*. Picture Player 2 on the right wing and Player 3 on the left wing. As soon as the ball is dribbled toward half-court, the wings switch places, so that Player 2 is now on the left, and Player 3 is on the right. This creates a lot of movement on the floor and will make the defense chase after their respective players, giving the dribbler an opportunity to drive to the basket or freeing up the wings to receive passes as the defense scrambles to keep up. The exchange can be a V-cut toward and then away from the basket (see diagram above right).

4. V-cut.

In this solution the wing steps into the defender, backing him up, and then cuts away. He will be open for a moment.

Above Left: Cutting to the Basket and creating movement on the court.

Above Right: Exchanging Wings.

Problem: The Other Team Is Stealing Your Team's Dribbles

You may find that the other team's players are simply quicker defensively, and that your team isn't protecting the ball well and isn't handling the defensive pressure.

Solution:

1. Work on your screens.

If your players are having trouble bringing the ball up because the defense is quick and the person with the ball is under extreme pressure, your players should try to pass it early and then screen on the ball to help take the pressure off the person under pressure (for more on screening see Pass and Screen Away drill **07**). As you work on the dribbling drills—crossover and stop and go—changing your pace to accelerate your dribble, also drill your players on screening the ball to free the dribbler. By drilling often on this, screening for each other will become much more intuitive for your offensive players.

2. Switch around your players.

If you have a point guard dribbling the ball and her defender is much quicker or better skilled, have your guard pass to another player. Sometimes there will be a really big player on the other team who will stand under the basket and be a problem for your team. Take whoever he's guarding and make him defend on the outside. Most of the big kids aren't as mobile as the smaller ones, so if you have a shorter player opposing this tall opponent, turn it into an advantage by letting your offensive player dribble the ball down the floor.

It's simply a matter of changing assignments. It's an advantage with all the drill work you do—the give-and-go, the pass and screen away, and the cut—that everyone should really be interchangeable. So if you're in a position where your best dribbler is having trouble against a very good defender, have someone else come out who may have a bigger, slower player guarding him, and let that player dribble the ball down the floor to initiate the offense.

Problem: Your Team Isn't Scoring Enough Points

Your players are working hard out on the court and are improving their skills, but they just aren't getting the points they need to win.

Solution:

1. Work on the simplest way to score—the fast break.

The easiest way to score at the youth level is the fast break. Instead of worrying about set positions or too many of the offensive concepts, just go back to the basics and improve your fast-break skills.

If everyone on your team can handle the ball reasonably well, tell

---

Notes from the Floor When You Have a Fast-Breaking Team, Take Advantage of It

One year I had a high school team where every player was about the same height. They were really all guards, and we didn't have what you'd traditionally call forwards and centers. Because everyone could dribble the ball reasonably well, I decided that whoever got the rebound was the point guard and would start the fast break down the court, instead of making an outlet pass. The other four players knew that if they didn't get the rebound, they should turn and run, but we made them run wide. The person with the ball would have the space in the middle, and we became a great fast-breaking team with that concept. You may find that you have a team where everyone can handle the ball. If that's the case, instead of everyone waiting to make a pass out of the back court, whoever gets the rebound could start up the fast break. The other four people sprint toward the basket, keeping it wide down the floor, and your team can attack aggressively. Concentrate on perfecting the skills needed for the fast break, instead of trying to teach too many plays or too many concepts, and your team will improve its ability to score.

---

your players that whoever gets the rebound is the point guard and should dribble it from there. All four other players on the floor should turn and run wide down the floor. The person with the ball will have the space in the middle to get to the other end so your team can attack aggressively.

2. Offensive movement.

If your team is not fast enough for a fast break, run a simple give-and-go. Most kids can do that. Even if the team doesn't score a lot, at least the kids will be moving.

Problem: During Games Your Team Begins to Sag and Loses Momentum

Sometimes during the game you'll see that the team is floundering. What you really need is a basket to get the team revved up and get good things happening.

Solution:

Establish an offensive play like a pick and roll. Get your top two players in a position to run a pick and roll play (see diagram at right). This is a play you will have worked on extensively in practice, and one that your best players should be comfortable doing. Have Player 1 with the ball come right up by the top of the circle in the center of the floor. Have Player 2 come up to screen her for an easy score (see **08**).

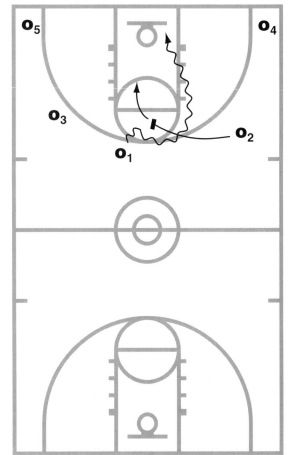

Pick and Roll.

Questions and Answers

Q. I have a player who has done very well in practice, but he has decided he doesn't want to play in the game. What should I do?

A. There could be many reasons why kids might not want to perform. Some may have a fear of failure, others may be getting pressure from their parents. They should come to the game anyway. Give this player an opportunity to play—call out his name and let him know you have him on the schedule to go in. If he says he doesn't want to play, say "Fine. It's a completely volunteer situation." Put another player in the position. Again, in the second half ask the player, "Are you ready to play? I've got you in with this unit." If he says no, say, "Okay. Hopefully next game you'll play." Don't put a lot of pressure on the situation. Don't give ultimatums. Try to nurture the player along, and work with his parents to lessen his fear of the game. A similar situation happened to me coaching a T-ball team this year. I had a player who just didn't want to bat. She'd play in the field but she just didn't want to hit. So we'd call her name out, and if she didn't get in line at her turn, the next person would go up. Toward the end of the year she started taking her turn. Then she got a hit, everybody cheered, and before you knew it, she ended up batting all the time. But it was a slow process, and this could happen in basketball as well.

Q. How do I ensure that the kids keep track of who they're guarding as the other team subs?

A. Teams can only substitute on a whistle—when the ball is not in play—so teach your kids to communicate every time a substitute enters the game. The player who is leaving the game should call out the number he is guarding and point to his man. A subbing player should always shake the hand of the person whom he is replacing and should ask which player he was guarding. This communication is extremely important to teach. You can simulate this situation in practice. Especially for the younger kids, the referees will wait to start play until everyone is ready.

Q. I have a huge team of 16 players, some with really difficult behavior issues. It would be a lot easier for me to divide them up into fairly permanent lines so that I don't have to worry too much about positions. Do I divide the players up into three lines of equal skill level or do I group the best kids together, essentially having a first, second, and third team? The better kids want to play with each other, but the lesser-skilled kids don't want to feel like they're third string.

A. Playing different combinations and having players of greater ability playing with those of lesser ability is crucial to kids' development. Set lines will also disrupt the way games are played because you will not be able to complement the arrangement of players on the opposing team.

Q. I have some players who can handle crossover moves, help-side defense, and the pick and roll, and others who can scarcely dribble and don't understand the 3-second rule. Help! How should I divide up my team for games?

A. During practice you are preparing to establish arrangements of player lineups and patterns of substitution. These will be crucial to the development of the players as individuals and members of a team. You need to create time each game in which the stronger players play together (probably 40 percent of the game on average); this is their time for maximum development and fun, and a coach must not be pressured into thinking that playing one's best players together is an act of poor sportsmanship. Thus, you need to allow time in practice for these players to play together. Have them compete against the players of lesser ability in a five-on-five situation and have them play two-on-two and three-on-three against each other. Games must also integrate players of different abilities. For means of competition and in order to keep some order and flow on the court, try to substitute at least one of your better players in with the players who struggle. Keep a frequent substitution pattern through the portions of the game in which you are integrating ability levels. Make sure that a portion of the game is played solely by your best players and that a bigger proportion of the game is played in this integrated arrangement.

Q. Do I play every team member equally, or do I play the more highly skilled kids somewhat more against the tougher teams? Every member feels great when we win. How do I resolve that conflict of playing to win yet making sure everyone participates and has a good time?

A. I really believe in my numbering system of substitution. If you stick with it consistently, it will solve all problems and get kids to root for each other. It is important to remember: winning isn't everything, but trying to win is. Many of the great lessons in basketball and in sports are learned in the pressure situations of close contests, not to mention the great joys experienced. It is a coach's job at your level to create these close games—blow-outs are not as helpful or as fun.

Q. We are about to go into our first game, and the other coach won't agree to a numbered substitution. He says he wants to win and will sub as necessary. Should I stick with my numbered plan or match his strategy so that my players aren't blown out?

A. The most important thing is to have your players involved in the game. Show your commitment to the philosophy that participation should be fair for all players, and go along with your original substitution plan. Believe me, you might not win the game, and there might be some down faces, but if you keep a positive attitude, you'll gain the respect not only of your players but of all the parents who have gone to the games as well. So in this situation, stick to your principles, stick to the philosophy, maintain good sportsmanship, and concentrate on your team.

Q. I made it clear that I expected my players to respect the referees and their decisions, but the ref we had at the first game was terrible and clearly didn't know some of the rules of the game. I didn't say anything at the time, but after the game my players had questions about the rules and the official. What do I tell them?

A. There are times when the officiating might be poor, but it is important for players to know that they are not to question calls. They must understand that mistakes may be made and that they all should be bigger than the situation. A coach should never allow players to complain about the officiating. There are plenty of other things on which the players should be concentrating. It's okay to say, "Well, you know, sometimes refs make mistakes, just as we all do. The real credit should be to you players who let her do her job. You kept your poise and showed her respect. That's something that is very noteworthy." Tell them that you also had a hard time, but by maintaining your cool you showed your respect for the game and the officials. Let them know that as players they did a good job. The main point of your conversation should be that no matter how bad they feel the officiating is during a game, lack of sportsmanship is never the answer.

Q. We won our first game, and after it was over some of my players were whooping and shouting. I was glad they were excited, but how much celebrating after a win is too much?

A. It's fine to be happy when you win, but you should work hard to get your players into a huddle right away after a game to channel the enthusiasm into good sportsmanship. Remember, when two teams play, one of the teams is going to be a losing team, and your winning players should respect exactly how the other team feels. Keep it low-key after you win, and keep it low-key after you lose. If you stay consistent with that and meet with your team, you'll prevent a lot of players from overindulging in the "whooping it up."

Q. One of my 8-year-olds just can't seem to understand that he is part of a team. Whenever he gets the ball he races down the court and fires up a shot from wherever he is when he's about to be stopped. I find myself screaming for him to pass it over and over the whole game, with no result.

A. Before the games and during the practice, emphasize the other aspects of the game. Talk about passing, rebounding, and defense as important components in addition to shooting. Encourage players who score to point to or in some way acknowledge those players who passed them the ball. That's really good for team chemistry, and it breeds unselfishness as well—once a player makes a basket, the attention is usually on the shooter. Turn it around so that the person who assisted is acknowledged.

Q. I have two players whose skill levels are well ahead of their teammates. The problem is, when they're in the game at the same time, they want to pass just to each other, and they completely dominate the play, leaving the other kids out of the action. What should I do?

A. You should make sure that in practice your best two players are competing against each other. In games, if you use the number system of substitution you can calculate the amount of times your best two players are on the court. When they are on the floor together, they will probably be more active and get more open than some of the others. In these situations it is fine for them to dominate play. Just make sure they don't always play together.

Q. We won our first game by a huge point margin. I'm proud of the kids, but I want to make sure they don't focus solely on winning. How do I address success?

A. Make sure that at your next practice, you go right back to the drill work. If you stay consistent in your practice format and focus on the importance of the drill work whether you win or you lose, the players will not lose focus on what the season is about. And next time this is happening in a game, try substituting in such a way as to facilitate a more closely matched score by mixing up the skill levels of the kids. In these situations you might not want to put all the best kids in together as much as you normally do. Though a close game is not always possible, particularly when one team is terribly overmatched, a coach can have a great influence in creating these pressure-packed, exciting, and fun game experiences for everyone involved.

Q. During the game our team completely fell apart, and I panicked. How can I make sure it doesn't happen again?

A. First, don't feel alone—this is very common for coaches when they see the ball being turned over and the score just getting out of control. The next time this happens, take a deep breath, bring the team in, and talk to them. Try to calm them down and then tell them just to play and not worry about the score. Give them something specific to work on, and when in doubt, stick to the basics. It will also be easier for you in a game situation if you prepare for how you will act if things don't go well. Make this a part of your game plan.

Q. Our team lost in a huge way. The kids worked hard and played well, but we were simply outmatched. They are feeling discouraged. How can I get them back on track and excited again?

A. Now is the time to really incorporate fun and games at practice. Reinforce their skills by doing such drills as dribble tag, relays with the baskets made, some shooting drills, some three-on-three competition where you keep score, and the combination transition drill where you get up to three-player combination transition drills. Get them moving and playing—the more they're moving and playing the game, the less they'll even think about any experience where they lost. Just get them involved and get them active, and be certain to emphasize what they did right.

CHAPTER 8

Dealing with Parents and Gender Issues

Perspective on Parents

Coaches have to realize that it is nearly impossible for parents to properly evaluate their own child's ability. I know this firsthand—I'm a parent, I have two boys playing college basketball and a third son playing youth-league sports—and I've also seen it throughout my thirty years of coaching. We all love our kids, we talk about them in glowing terms, and we wish that everything would go right for them, regardless of the sport. If it's Little League baseball, you wish they would get a hit every time, and you hate to see them strike out. If they're playing basketball, you want every shot to go in and every rebound to be theirs. You want them to do well so they'll feel as good about themselves as you do. The problem is that parents just can't be as realistic about their children's abilities as a coach can—and you will need to understand and appreciate that as a coach. Situations are bound to arise where you will have to address a parent's expectations versus the reality of the situation, but the key is to communicate, and in a very direct manner.

The main thing in dealing with parents, without question, is to keep the lines of communication open. Don't detour from your philosophy as a coach and what you want out of the program. Keep all the principles in mind when you're dealing with parents. There may be times when you disagree and when you'll have to tell the parent that you disagree with what they are saying. Explain that you are running the program your way, and hope that they'll come around and understand your viewpoint.

It's also good to have some kind of ongoing communication with parents. Regular letters sent home throughout the season can cover logistics, schedule changes, reminders to bring water every week, or whatever. You can use these communications to offer an upbeat tone about the team, no matter how well the team is doing in games. Some kind of fun potluck dinner at midseason is also a great way to maintain communication, enabling you to have contact with the parents other than just when they are unhappy about something.

Be Organized at All Times

Many potential misunderstandings between coaches and parents are caused by a lack of organization on the coaches' part—perhaps the coaches haven't been clear about their expectations for the season or about their coaching, playing, and substitution philosophy. You will need to make sure that you are well organized and are communicating your expectations clearly and openly through the letter you send at the beginning of the season and the atmosphere you create with the players. Parents appreciate this honesty and mutual respect.

Help Parents Look at the Big Picture

Parents need to realize that there are many players on your team, and that your interest and concern is for all of them, not for one or two. You may occasionally have parents whose expectation levels are so high that if their children aren't excelling on the court immediately after joining the team, there is something wrong with the coach and the program. You may need to remind parents that everyone has a beginning step, and to encourage them to judge the progress not so much on productivity or success during the game but by how much the players are enjoying the game and learning new skills. Sometimes parents have to be reminded that the success of their children is measured by the improvement in their skills and their continued high interest and enthusiasm in the game.

Addressing Gender Issues

When you're dealing with young kids, my philosophy has always been that the fewer rules in regard to gender issues, the better. Kids in particular have a real way of sorting things out. If I have a coed team and say to a group of players, "Everybody pair up and get a ball," it's very likely that the top two players will be paired up, and if we have a couple of weaker players, there's a good chance they will be paired up. If we have six girls we will probably look at three sets of partners where the girls will pair up to do these drills. That just happens—kids don't necessarily take gender into account when they are choosing partners for drills, they choose the person most like them in ability. Try to let your players sort themselves out, regardless of gender— you will probably find that players of like ability will match up.

Each situation may be different, but if you just let things happen and not create an issue out of something that isn't one to your players, everybody becomes comfortable with whatever situation works out. With the younger kids, try and encourage a variety of different groupings. Whether people are right-handed or left-handed, whatever their race, whether they are male or female, the principles of being a team—playing together, not criticizing each other, and supporting one another—should be paramount.

Girls tend to take criticism very personally, and they also want to know the rationale behind a particular drill or skill, whereas most boys I've coached would run through a wall if I told them to and wouldn't question why they were doing it. You won't have to change any drills or your coaching philosophy. Just be prepared to offer girls more information and probably a bit more direction. You'll find that the girls are just as competitive as boys and often much more coachable. It's all in how you bring that competitive spirit out in them.

That being said, whereas younger kids often compete against each other across gender up to the sixth or seventh grade, by then teams should be single gender if possible. Otherwise, boys tend to dominate the play, and the differences in the learning styles for girls and boys, as well as their emotional differences, make it a good idea to put them on separate teams. Girls and boys are motivated in different ways, so what works with the girls may fail miserably with the boys. Athletics is a natural place for girls to develop confidence and assertive behavior, and by junior high the presence of boys can diminish the experience—maybe not for all girls or in every situation, but certainly for some. By this age, sports should be separate from the boy-girl stuff that will certainly be starting for many kids, making them self-conscious with the opposite gender.

Questions and Answers

Q. I have some parents who keep giving their kids "advice" about their performance after games and practices, but I really disagree with their suggestions. How do I address this?

A. The easiest way to address it is to realize that coaches aren't going to change how parents bring up their kids, nor should they try to. The real issue here is how is the young player relating to your coaching? Your concern is whether he's doing the things that you want. If his parents' advice affects his performance or behavior with the team, then it has to be addressed. But we really can't tell parents how to bring up their children.

Q. Some parents insist on sitting right behind the bench and making comments during the game about the other team and the refereeing. I know they are trying to be supportive to the kids and the team, but I don't like it. What's a diplomatic solution here?

A. Preparation is the key to this kind of situation. In your preseason letter to parents you need to talk about the importance of sportsmanship and to emphasize that good sportsmanship is to be exemplified not only by the players but by the parents and coach as well. Prepare them to act like good sports by setting a standard yourself that's very high.

Q. I have a parent who constantly questions my judgment about how much time each team member plays. She feels that her child, who is quite good, is not playing enough. I have explained that it is important for every team member to play, regardless of ability. We simply don't see eye-to-eye on this, and the parent cannot accept my explanation.

A. You should respectfully agree to disagree, as simple as it sounds, and stick to your own philosophy and principles.

Q. I have a parent who is incredibly critical of his child. He has a negative way of shouting orders to this child when she's playing and then instructs her when she's on the bench about how she should have done something differently. How can I diplomatically ask the parent to back off and adopt a more positive attitude?

A. It's important that you get the parent to respect what you're trying to do as a coach and tell him it's confusing if too many people are coaching during time on the court. Inform the parent that you are the coach, and you'd like your players to listen to only one voice and to respond to one stimulus on the court.

With this problem, as well as with other difficult situations involving parents, the most important advice I can offer is to address the problem immediately. Don't be shy about speaking up. Send a letter home after a couple of games, reminding parents in general what you're expecting from them and identifying specifically the problems you're seeing. If you don't get the desired change in behavior, speak to the parents directly.

Q. My team has only one girl on it. She seems very comfortable and confident with the boys, but some of the boys are not comfortable with her. What should I do?

A. Constantly reinforce the principle that everyone's the same on the team, regardless of gender, height, skill level, or anything else. The more you stress the importance of valuing each individual on the team, the more your boys will accept and appreciate this message. Find something that this girl does well and praise her for it. Make sure that the boys are aware that she contributes to the team.

Q. I have a team of both boys and girls. In the drills the girls always tend to partner with girls and the boys with boys, rather than pairing up by equal skill level. Should I let them do this, or pair them by skill level regardless of gender?

A. You should certainly let them pair up by skill level or gender, however they're comfortable. Players make decisions and sort them out quite well. However, if players aren't learning the skills or are having trouble because their skill levels are uneven, give them some time to try it together and then mix up the pairings to give everyone a new partner. This will allow your players some autonomy but will also solve uneven skill problems if they arise.

Q. The boys on my team always hog the ball. They consistently pass only to other boys, ignoring the girls. What should I do?

A. There are several suggestions:
1. Create a two-on-two tournament drill in practice, each team composed of a boy and a girl. If there's an imbalance of boys, put two weaker boys together.
2. Practice and implement into your games specifically designed plays in which boys and girls have different roles and must pass to each other. Call out these plays in the game if boys aren't passing to girls.
3. Take the particular boys aside privately and speak to them individually about the matter, emphasizing the concept of team and reminding them that one of the ways to earn playing time on the team is to pass to all available teammates.

Q. Some of the strategies I use with the girls work really well, but the boys don't seem to respond.

A. You need to expect that some kids will not respond to certain methods or drills, and thus you need to teach in a variety of ways. You will encounter such a problem with a team of all boys or all girls as well, and you need to alter drills or concepts in order to try and reach each player. Consequently, plan relatively short and frequently changing drills.

PART TWO

Drills: The Foundation for Growth, Happiness, and a Coach's Peace of Mind

CHAPTER 9

Fundamental Drills

Warming Up

Quick Jumps F1

This jump is similar to the motion of jumping rope. Players make short, quick, stationary jumps, keeping their hands over their heads. Each time they jump up, they should reach their hands up high. As they hit the ground, they immediately push off again. Their hands should never go below their shoulders. When you blow the whistle, players begin jumping. After a minute or two, yell, "Right foot only!" Get them to do 10 or 15

Diagram Key. Corresponding players on opposite teams have the same number (e.g., X_3 and O_3). See also the court terminology diagram on page 13.

●	start	®	rebound
├──■	pick, screen	□	jump stop
──▶	running	□□	one-two stop
- - -▶	pass	▲	cone
∿∿∿▶	dribble	1 2 3 4 5	line of players
⌐ ⌐ ⌐▶	bounce pass	❶ ❷ ❸	order of events
↰	pivot	**C**	coach
◀───▶	crossover move	X_1	defensive player
⊝──▶	shot	O_1	offensive player
╱╱	cut, taking a step forward and back	$X_a X_b$	player a, player b

jumps and then yell, "Left foot!" Then go back to both. Encourage players and remind them to keep their hands over their heads: "That's good! That's good! Quick jumps! Hands over the head! Quick jumps!" 👉

Power Jumps F2

Players stand with bent knees and bring their hands down below their knees. Then they explode upward, popping their knees and sending their hands straight up into the air. Players' entire bodies—their heads, knees, shoulders, arms—explode up to the top. Then they gather themselves together and power jump again. Encourage them to use their arms for propulsion: "Throw the hands through the ceiling! Throw them right through!" They will probably manage to do this for only 20 or 30 seconds. 👉

Donkey Jumps F3

This warm-up drill calls for your players to jump up and kick their heels right up to their buttocks. You may need to demonstrate this jump to your team. As soon as players do five or six donkey jumps, start mixing in other jumps. 👉

Foot Fire F4

This drill will help your players learn to get their feet moving. Have the team spread out. They should bend their knees and flex at the waist. At your signal players move from foot to foot as quickly as possible. Demonstrate this if necessary. Use hand or voice signals to have them do turns. If you point to the left or yell, "Left," they're going to jump a quarter turn to the left and then jump back. If you point or yell, "Up," they jump. Make a game of it, turning them to the right and left and jumping up, and keep it going for a minute or more. 👉

Dribbling

The following skill benchmarks will help teach your players to dribble.

Skill 1: Dribbling While Stationary

Stationary Dribble F5

Spread out your players around the court, each with a basketball. Players bend their knees, flex at the waist, and begin by bouncing the ball with the preferred hand. Make sure they aren't slapping at the ball. Encourage your players to pound the ball to the floor to develop the muscles of the fingers and the wrist. 👉

Heads-Up F6

As your players are dribbling, tell them that you will put your hands in the air and show different numbers of fingers. Players are to call out the number of fingers they see. This drill makes them keep their heads up while concentrating on pushing the ball to the floor.

Crossover Move (Switch Hands) F7

Now have your players switch to the nonpreferred hand to dribble. They will notice a difference in ability with this hand. Continue to do the Heads-Up drill with players dribbling with the nonpreferred hand. Now have your players turn their hand to the outside of the ball and push to the inside, so that they dribble the ball across their body to the other hand. Have them dribble right to left, then left to right, as they practice dribbling with the hand on the side of the ball. If they move their hands to the inside of the ball and push outward, they are practicing an offensive move known as the *inside-out dribble*.

Skill 2: Dribbling While Moving

Moving Dribble F8

Line up your players on the sideline facing across the court. When you yell, "Go," all players move across the court, dribbling with the preferred hand. Whenever you whistle, they must come to a stop. When you whistle again, they begin their moving dribble again. Have them work with both the preferred and nonpreferred hand.

Whistle F9

Line up your players on the sideline facing across the court. When you yell, "Go," all players dribble, with the preferred hand, across the court. Whenever you whistle, they must come to a jump stop. When players reach the other side and reverse direction, they must dribble with the nonpreferred hand. After they learn how to stop, players should change direction on your whistle and change dribble hands every time they change direction.

Dribble Tag F10

Dribble tag is a great game that also promotes dribbling skills. Everyone, including the coach, has a ball while practicing dribbling. You are "it," and while dribbling, you try to tag a player, who becomes "it." If a less skilled player is having trouble tagging someone, make sure she can tag you. You may notice during this drill that all of your players are dribbling with the preferred hand. Play the game again, this time requiring your players to dribble with the nonpreferred hand.

Steal-the-Ball F11

Have all your players dribble while at the same time trying to knock away their teammates' balls. When a player's ball is knocked out of bounds, he is out of the game. This game teaches players to protect the ball while dribbling.

Dribble Relays F12

Another game that reinforces moving dribbling skills is relay races. Divide up your players into pairs and have them practice speed dribbles. Vary the distance of the races by using the lines of the court. Always have them jump-stop and hand the ball to their teammates.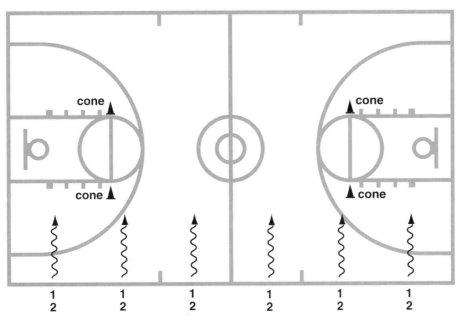

Skill 3: Changing Speed and Direction While Dribbling

Stop-and-Go F13

Set up four cones, one on each side of each foul line (see diagram below). Have your players line up and dribble to the cones. Every time they come to a cone they stop moving but continue dribbling. They then immediately accelerate to the next cone.

Stop-and-Go drill

Full-Court Stop and Dribble F14

Players form two lines; everyone has a ball and is dribbling. When you blow the whistle, the players start down the court. At the whistle they stop and dribble in place. Have them go down the court dribbling with their right hands and come back dribbling left-handed.

Skill 4: Learning Offensive Dribbling Moves

Stop-and-Cross F15

Line your players up on the sideline facing the other side of the court. They should dribble across the floor to the middle of the court and do a *stop-and-go*, which is basically coming to a jump stop, keeping the dribble alive, crossing over, and continuing. They will then come back dribbling left-handed and do a stop-and-go on the sideline. Emphasize the crossover, demonstrating it again if you need to. Remember to emphasize a low, hard dribble, coming to a stop in the center of the floor, and a crossover from one hand to the other hand. Continue dribbling with the other hand back to the sideline. (Tim Hardaway of the Miami Heat is known for his nasty crossover. Tell your players to work on theirs to be like his: they'll get excited about doing the same moves as professional players.)

Passing

Partner Passing F16

On your whistle, players pair up around the gym, approximately 6 to 8 feet apart (or farther, if your players are older). Have them work on a series of passes, beginning with the chest pass. Remind them to step to the target, pushing their thumbs down, and follow through to the target. Move on to the bounce pass and overhead pass. It doesn't have to be a long drill. Move fairly quickly through the different types of passes. If you find players are having trouble with strength and "snapping" the ball off, concentrate on just one-hand passing and work on pushing through to the target. This is called a one-handed push pass. Players should move farther apart as they develop strength and confidence.

Dribble Passing F17

Using the same pattern as above, have your players dribble the ball three times, then pass. This makes the drill more gamelike.

Pass-Receive F18

If you don't have enough balls for all of your players to do the dribble-pass drill, or if you want to keep everyone moving, set up two lines about 20 feet apart (see diagram at left). The two lines should face each other. The player with the ball passes it to her receiver and then runs to the end of the receiving line. The receiver passes to the next person in the opposite line. As the players move through the lines, yell out different kinds of passes. This can also be used as a great warm-up drill, since it gets your kids moving, listening, and working on catching and passing.

Pass-Receive drill

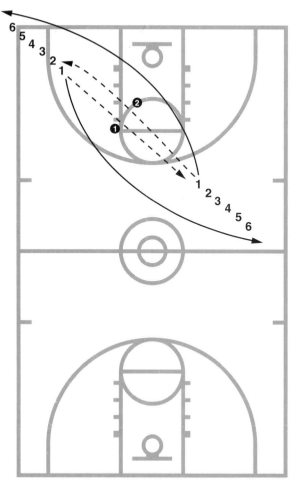

Catching

Catching is an art that takes concentration and hard work to develop. These three intermediate-level drills will help your players develop their catching skills.

Soft Hands F19

To develop soft hands, or a touch and a feel for the ball, have your players catch the ball with one hand, putting the other hand behind their backs. Make sure the passers don't throw too hard. To help them develop soft hands, or a feel for the ball, have your players catch the ball with one hand, putting the other hand behind their backs. Receiving the ball with one hand also increases the player's concentration and focus on the catching motion. Make sure the passers don't throw too hard. The catchers should be able to catch the ball softly and rest the ball on their fingertips. If the player's hands are too small to catch it with one hand, have them pick up the pace a bit, so that the passes between the two partners are quicker and the players are snapping their wrists and using their fingertips to "tap" the ball back and forth—keeping the ball in control without cradling it with their bodies. The catchers are be forced to cradle the ball—they have to release the ball as it comes to them in order to catch it with one hand, since their hands are so small. Receiving the ball with one hand also increases the player's concentration and focus on the catching motion. ☞ → ☞

Anticipating the Pass F20

It is important for receivers to always anticipate the pass, from wherever it might come. Have your receivers turn their backs to the person passing. When the passer makes a call, the receiver turns around, and the ball is passed. This drill is especially effective for increasing concentration because players have to learn to react immediately to a ball on its way. ☞

Bad Pass F21

This is a drill that you should do with all your players, if possible. Throw a hard underhand or overhand pass that is too low, too high, or too left—basically, a bad pass. These bad passes will help your players react to difficult passes, in-crease their concentration, and develop the soft hands needed for catching. ☞

Stopping and Pivoting

The following drills will help your players learn to stop and pivot effectively.

Jump-Stop Left-Right and Right-Left F22

This is a group pivoting drill that you can do in either the whole or half of the gym (see page 106). Have your players form a square with everyone facing the same direction. When you blow the whistle, the players run around the square.

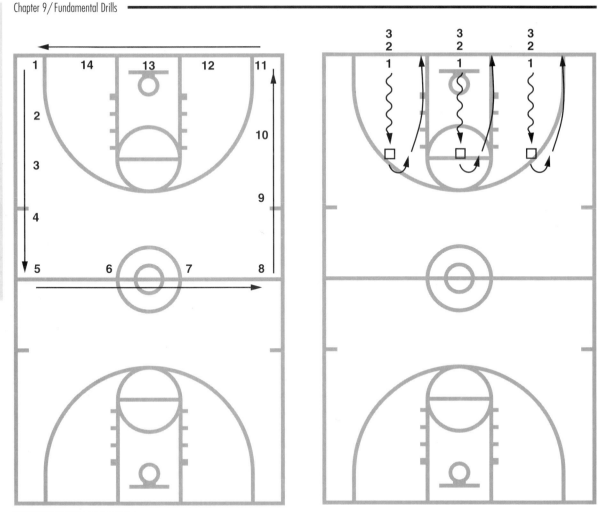

Left: Jump-Stop Left-Right and Right-Left drill

Right: Dribbling Whistle Pivot drill

When you blow the whistle again, they must come to a one-two stop. The foot that hits first will be their pivot foot. You then tell them to pivot— quarter turn, full circle, back to the front. When everyone is facing the same direction, blow the whistle and do the drill again.

Two-Footed Stop F23

At your whistle, have your players run slowly around the same square as used for practicing the one-two stop in the Jump-Stop Left-Right and Right-Left drill. This time, when you whistle again, they do a jump stop with two feet. You tell them which foot is the pivot foot and then tell them to pivot— quarter turn, full circle, back to the front. As above, when everyone is facing the same direction, blow the whistle and do the drill again.

Dribbling Whistle Pivot F24

Divide your players into three or four lines on the end line (see diagram above right). Everyone should have a ball. Those players waiting in line should practice their dribbling while waiting for their turn. When you whistle, the first player in each line takes off, dribbling down the floor. When you whistle again, the players come to a jump stop, catching the dribble. You yell, "Pivot!" and they pivot around their pivot foot and run back to the end line. The next group starts when the first group returns. 🏀

Dribble, Jump-Stop, Pivot, Pass   F25

Have your players line up in three or four lines (see diagram at right). The first player in each line dribbles out with the right hand to a line on the court, comes to a jump stop, pivots around, and dribbles back with the left hand. At your whistle, they stop and pass to the next person in line; then they run to the back of the line. 🏀

Combination   F26

This drill combines dribbling, passing, catching, and pivoting (see diagram below). Divide your players into partners and spread them out the width of the court from end line to end line. They should have one ball for every two people. The person with the ball dribbles out and comes to a jump stop, *facing away from* their target receiver. Then the passer pivots around and makes a chest

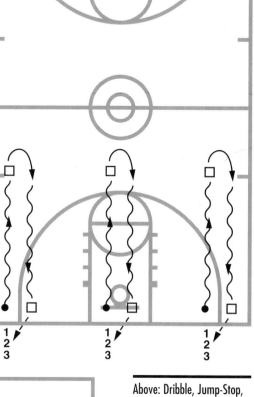

Above: Dribble, Jump-Stop, Pivot, Pass drill

Left: Combination drill

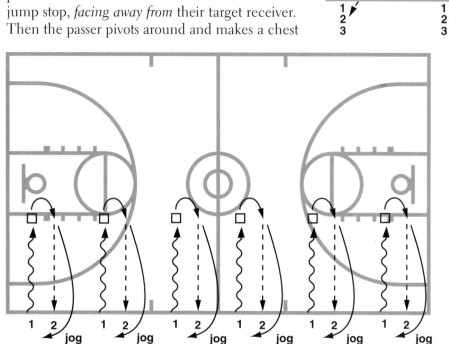

pass to the receiver. After making the pass, the player runs behind the team-mate while the teammate dribbles out 15 feet, makes a jump stop, pivots, and throws a chest pass back to the original player. Do this drill with all the various passes. It's a nice way to incorporate all the skills learned in each individual drill.

Shooting

The Layup F27

Players start dribbling with the preferred hand. A right-handed player starts on the right side of basket, taking his first step with his right leg. Then his left leg plants and acts as the jumping leg. The player drives his right knee up in the air, puts his hand behind the ball, and extends his hand. Therefore, the rhythm and footwork of a right-handed layup is the follow-ing: right leg down, left leg down, right knee up. For the left-handed layup, starting on the left side of the basket, it is left leg down, right leg down, left knee up.

Getting the right distance from the hoop when shooting is crucial: if the player gets too close, she gets under the hoop, which takes away the angle. A good way to get the right amount of distance on a layup is to start the first step at the block in the lane. When going in for the shot, players should extend their arm upward as they drive up to the basket, releasing the ball at the highest point.

Baskets have squares painted behind them on the backboard. Players should lay the ball up in the back corner so the ball hits the square and goes through the basket—it is important for the player to lay up the ball in the corner, not the center, of the square.

Driving the knee up in the air helps a player to jump high, rather than long—if players are speed dribbling down the floor and take a layup without driving up the knee, they will keep going forward rather than up toward the basket. This is a problem area for many kids.

Layup Rhythm F28

If you find your players are having trouble getting the rhythm of driving to the basket, stop them and slow down the process. Have them take one step with the right foot, one with the left, then drive the right knee into the air (or the opposite motions for left-handed shooters). Doing this over and over will help them develop the right rhythm. As they become more comfortable with the rhythm, have them try the motions with the ball in their hands and then with one dribble at the outset.

Teaching from the nonpreferred side is much more difficult but also important. Using the same drill, right-handed shooters should dribble with their left hand and step left, right, then drive the left knee up into the air; left-handed shooters should do the opposite motions.

Layup Strength F29

This drill helps players develop strength for layups. Using either a wall or the backboard, players stand with the preferred hand behind the ball, extend the hand, shoot the ball, and then catch the rebound. They should also practice this drill with the nonpreferred hand. Doing this drill over and over will markedly improve your players' strength within a week or so. The rest is all rhythm.

Pull-Up F30

This drill is similar to the layup drill, but here your players will pull up and do a jump stop at a medium distance from the basket and shoot, pushing off with both feet. The reason for this is that when the other team's defenders are waiting by the basket, your players will have to pull up before shooting.

Note that players will sometimes get bored with layups, especially as their skills advance. If so, keep challenging them by giving them different layup drills. For example, have them do a left-handed layup on the right side or a right-handed layup on the left side. Or they might do an underneath right-handed hook, where rather than extending his arm up and in toward the basket, the player swings his arm out and over his head toward the basket in a "hooking" arc. Another option is to try a reverse layup, where the player will come in under the basket as if he were going to do a traditional layup, then go under the basket and lay up the ball on the other side of the net, with his back to the backboard.

Two-Line Layup drill

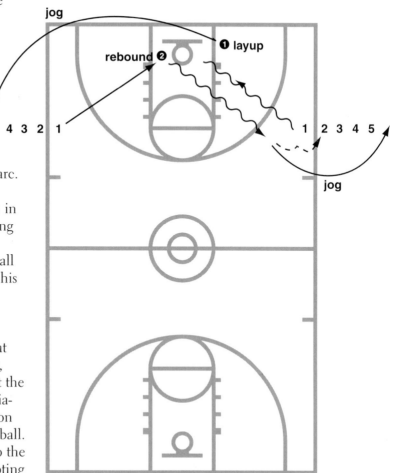

Two-Line Layup F31

Divide your players into two lines at one end on either side of the court, starting on the outside of the key at the imaginary extended foul line(see diagram at right). The line of players on the right side of the basket has the ball. The player with the ball dribbles to the basket and makes a layup (see shooting

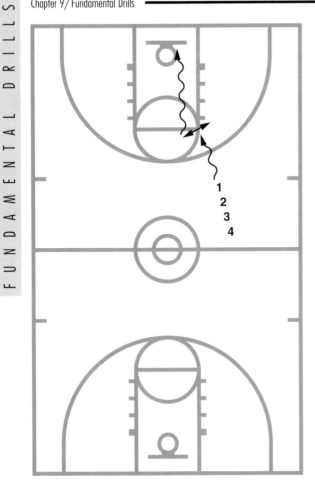

1
2
3
4

Crossover Layup drill

fundamentals on pages 32–34), while the first player on the left line will get the rebound, dribble back to the shooting line, and pass to the next shooter. The first players will go to the end of the opposite line. Every person should get four or five of these shots before you move to the next drill. ☞

Crossover Layup   F32

From the same starting position as the Two-Line Layup drill, have your players dribble to the *elbow*, the corner of the foul line, and do a crossover move for a layup (see diagram at left). ☞

Combination Layup   F33

Divide your players into two lines facing each other, starting at the foul line (see page 111). Everyone holding a ball should stand in the passing line, and the other players are in the shooting line. The first person with a ball starts dribbling to the elbow. As soon as she does that, she looks at her teammate (called "reading" her teammate)—the player starting without a ball who is also moving to the elbow. The receiver lets the passer know she is ready to receive the ball by raising her hand up to show her palm. The passer steps, snaps, extends. The receiver catches the ball and gets her balance. If she is coming from right to left, her right foot will be her pivot foot as she catches the ball. After she catches the ball and goes *knee to knee*—comes to a one-two stop and does a swing step by swinging her front leg over to the basket—she bounces the ball, extends her left foot toward the basket, and takes a layup shot. After the shot is taken, the shooter rebounds her own basket, and the two players go to the ends of the opposite lines. Then the next two players complete the drill, on down the lines (see page 107). ☞

Two-Line Layup Back-Cut   F34

You can create many variations of this drill to enhance different skills. For example, the player receiving the ball pretends he isn't open and makes a *back-cut*—he cuts back to the basket. The person dribbling will see that the receiver hasn't signaled that he's open, watches the back-cut, and snaps off a bounce pass to the receiver at his signal. The receiver then goes into a layup. ☞

Shooting Progression F35

Another variation on shooting drills is to practice shooting from various spots on the court. Divide your players into two groups, starting on the foul line extended to the sideline. One line has the ball and is the passing line, while the other group is the shooting line. This time when the receiver catches the ball, she squares to the basket (her shoulders and feet face the basket), bends her knees, extends her arms, and follows through to the target. You can run through this drill for three or four progressions. Start closer to the basket with younger players, and move as far out as the three-point line with older players.

Also from this formation players can catch the ball, make a fake, take one dribble to the right (or to the left) to clear, and then shoot off the dribble. A *shot fake* is a shot not taken, where the knees stay down while the ball comes up. A good fake will make the defense rise, giving the shooter another opportunity to clear the defense and score.

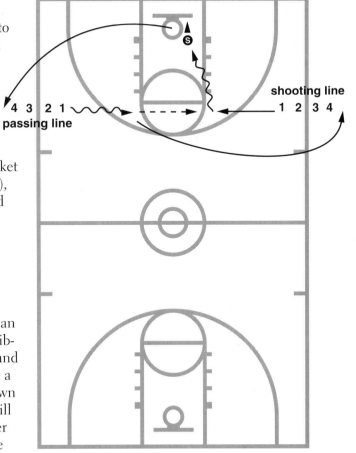

Combination Layup drill

After your players have learned the basics of this drill, you can allow them to choose their variations of the drill to practice. By doing this, they see that they have choices and have to make decisions during games. Make sure the players aren't doing the same moves all the time. This is a great drill for keeping everyone moving, for focusing on what's happening on the court, and for teaching all the players the basic concepts of the game. ☞

Shooting Competition F36

Use both baskets (see page 112). Divide the players into equal numbers of three-, four-, or five-person teams, one ball per team, and line them up at the elbows. The first person in each line has a ball and shoots once. If he makes the basket, the whole team counts the number "One!" loudly. The shooter gets his rebound, passes it to the next player in line, and moves to the end of the line. When the next basket goes in, the whole team yells, "Two!" Play to seven hoops—the first team that makes seven baskets sits down so that all the other teams know who is the winner. If there is time,

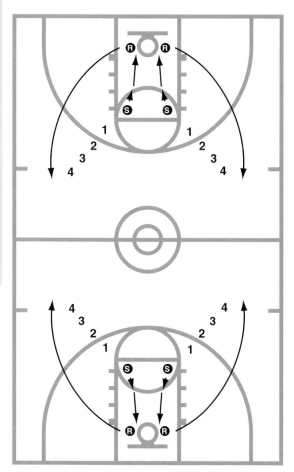

Shooting Competition

players can rotate positions and do the shooting competition again.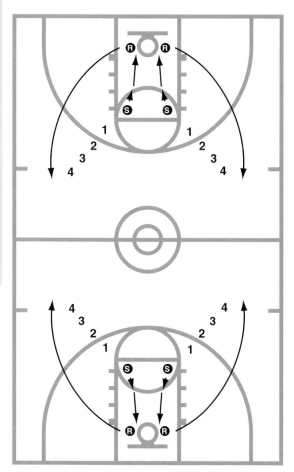

Free Throw Shooting F37

The advantage of taking a free throw is that there is no defense crowding the player, who has 10 seconds in which to take a free shot. To practice free throws, players line up at the foul line to take their shots. The shooter should find the air hole in the ball and place her index finger across the seam just below that hole. This technique will help players develop a good shooting position. As they shoot, remind them to pop their knees, extend their arms, and follow through to their target. 🔵 → 🔵

Dribble Shoot Relay F38

This game is a great ending activity. Divide your players into four groups. Line them up behind the basket at one end. The only way they can score is to dribble the entire length of the floor, take one shot at the basket at the other end, and then dribble all the way back to their team. Again, if someone on the team makes a layup, the whole team will count "One!" The first team that makes seven baskets sits down. The losing groups have to do sit-ups. If there is time, play the game again with players using the nonpreferred hand to dribble. 🔵

Rebounding

Mirror F39

This is a basic defense drill, but you can also use it to introduce the basic steps in rebounding. When you say, "I'm a shooter and I shoot," the players should put a hand up to contest the shot, turn, stay low, and pretend to box out their particular man. For more information about mirroring, see pages 43–44 and **D3** 🔵

Toss off the Backboard F40

This is a good drill for teaching young players to actually get up and grab the ball at its highest peak. Have two lines at the elbow facing the hoop at both ends of the court. The coach (and assistant) will each throw the ball off the backboard, and the first player in each line jumps up to catch the ball when it bounces off the backboard. Stress the idea of getting up and going to the ball. When the player lands, he should yell, "Ball!" It is important that when the player lands he is strong and secure with the ball.

One-on-One Toss off the Backboard F41

This is a variation of the drill above. Here, there is only one line on the end line. In this drill, the first player in line is a token offensive player at the wing or block position, and the second player is the defensive rebounder. The coach stands at the foul line with the ball. The defender should be denying the ball in a good defensive stance. As the coach shoots the ball (throwing it softly off the backboard), the defender yells, "Shot!" makes contact with her man, turns and pushes her hips backward into the offensive player (boxing out), and then jumps up to receive the ball. The two players switch positions and run through the drill a second time. Then they go to the end of the line, and the next two players go through the drill.

After the players have a good grasp of boxing out a stationary player, have the players play live when the shot goes up, with the offensive player aggressively going for the rebound against the defender. Stress the idea of making contact and boxing out to prevent the offensive player from getting closer to the basket.

Two-on-Two Toss off the Backboard F42

This is the same drill as above except that a second offensive player and defender are added. The defensive players should be in the deny position, and when the coach shoots, the players should aggressively try for the rebound.

This drill can be made more competitive by dividing the players into teams of two. A point is scored if the defense gets the rebound. The defenders stay on defense until the offense gets the ball. At that point, the offense becomes the defense, and another team comes in on offense. You can score points only on defense by getting the rebound. The first team to reach five rebounds wins.

CHAPTER 10

Offensive Drills

Shot and Pass Fakes

Dribble Jump-Stop Drill with Fake 01

Divide your players into two lines, starting at the foul line and extending to each sideline. Just one line has balls. Player A dribbles to the basket, does a jump stop, and makes a shot fake and then a real shot. Player B rebounds the ball, and both players jog to the end of the opposite line. A variation of this drill is to have the two lines farther apart. Player A dribbles toward Player B, does a jump stop, does a pass fake to Player B, and then makes a real pass. Again, both players go to the end of the opposite line. 👉

Ball Fake Game 02

This game uses five players, but you can vary the numbers to accommodate the size of your team. You can have two or more groups playing this game at once. With five players, three are on offense (one on each wing and one at the top of the key), and two are on defense (one at each elbow). The offensive players pass the ball around the perimeter to each other (no dribbling) while the defensive players try to steal or get a hand on the ball. The defense receives a point when either defender touches the ball; the offense receives a point when they get a defender to lunge after a pass that is faked by an offensive player. This teaches *convincing* ball fakes, and players enjoy the chance to fake out a teammate. 👉

Two-Man Options to Teach Cutting and Moving Strategically

Back-Cut to Layup 03

Divide your players into two lines, starting at the foul line and extending to each sideline (see page 115). Just one line has balls. Player A dribbles at

Back-Cut to Layup drill

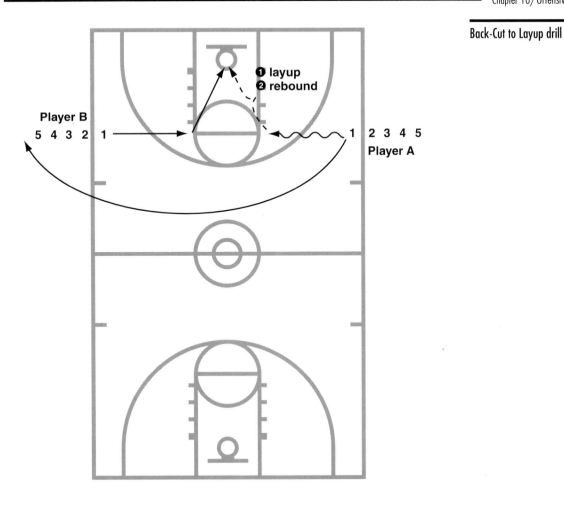

Player B. Player B takes a few steps toward Player A and then cuts to the basket. (In a game situation, if she was being closely guarded this might free her for a layup.) Player A bounce-passes to Player B, who takes a layup and gets her own rebound. Each player goes to the end of the opposite line. 🖎

Screen to Handoff 04

Divide your players into two lines, one at the point and one at the wing (see page 116). If Player A dribbles at Player B and Player B keeps coming, that means he wants to use Player A as a screener (a player who jumps in the path of the defender). Player B comes right up to Player A, shoulder to shoulder, and Player A can just hand him the ball. Player B continues to the basket for a layup, or he could step behind and take a shot. 🖎

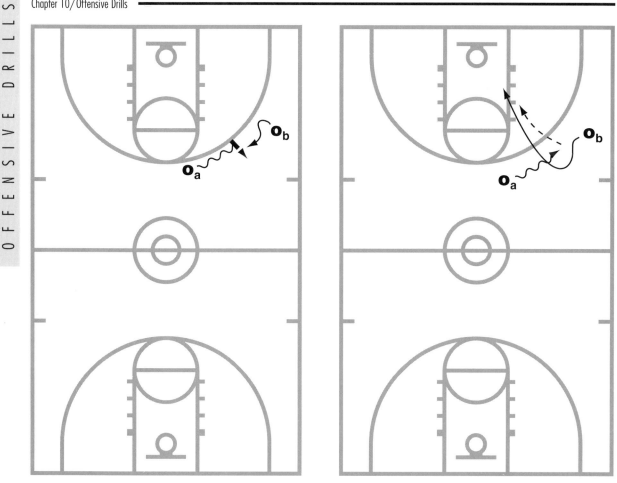

Above Left: Screen to Handoff drill

Above Right: Runaround drill

Runaround 05

If there is a defender between Player A and Player B preventing the hand-off, Player B should go around Player A and then cut to the basket to receive either an overhead pass or a bounce pass (see diagram above right). Going to the basket this way is called the "runaround."

Give-and-Go 06

The concept of give-and-go is really explained by its name: I give you the ball, and you give it back to me as I cut to the basket (see page 117). Again, the principle of moving at angles or taking two steps away from where we want to go before we get there is absolutely the same.

Divide your players into two lines, one at the top of the circle, the other at the wing. Player A, who is at the top of the circle, passes the ball to Player B, who is on the right wing. Player A takes two steps to the left, away from the ball, to give the defender the impression that she is moving away from the play. Then she plants off the outside foot and makes a hard-cut right to the basket. As soon as she's open, she should show her hands to Player B to give Player B an open target and to indicate that she is ready to receive a pass. Then Player B, who has the ball, returns the pass to Player A, who goes to the basket for a layup.

Player B rebounds the ball, dribbles all the way out to the top of the circle, and goes to the end of the shooting line. Player A, who made the give-and-go, now goes to the end of the receiving line. The next two players repeat the drill. You should do this drill from both sides of the floor.

Pass and Screen Away 07

The Pass and Screen Away drill is designed to free a teammate without the ball so that the player will become open to receive a pass (see page 118). In this play, rather than doing a give-and-go, Player A passes the ball and then moves to free his teammate by becoming a screen (getting between his teammate and the defender).

Put your players in two lines on the same side of the floor. Put a coach on the right side. Player B is on the left wing, and Player A is at the top of the key. There are several steps to this drill:

1. Player A passes the ball to the coach on the right side.

2. Player A then moves to set a screen against Player B's (pretend) defender, jumping into the position with both feet so that she isn't moving.

3. Player B, moving at the same time as Player A, takes two steps toward the end line and then cuts to the basket, looking for a return pass from the coach.

A good guideline for setting up a screen is to set the screen right where the defender is rather than where the offensive player is. Ideally the screener should jump into the screen. He should call Player B's name

Give-and-Go drill

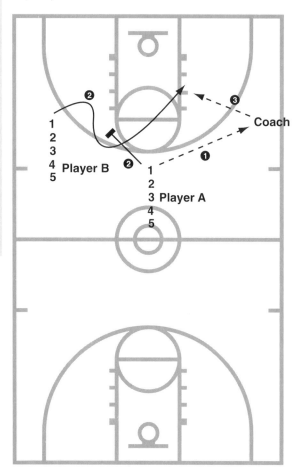

Pass and Screen Away drill

and say, "Use me, Jimmy!" or "Use me, Sally!" so that the person with the ball knows his only choice is to drive to the basket or look at the person who passed the ball to him. Sometimes the passer does a give-and-go, as described above; other times the passer tries to free a teammate.

Pick and Roll 08
The pick and roll is a play designed to help free a person with the ball so that the player can either drive to the basket for a layup or pass to another open player. Put your players in two lines on the same side of the floor. Player A, at the top of the key, and Player B, on the right wing, follow these steps:

1. Player A passes the ball to Player B.

2. After passing, Player A jumps in to screen Player B, who now has the ball. Player A calls, "Use me, Sarah!" or "Use me, Bobby!" to let her know the screen is coming.

3. Player B makes a jab step one way and then comes back off the screen, *shoulder to shoulder* with Player A (see sidebar page 119).

If the defense gets caught in the screen, Player B, the dribbler, should go all the way for a layup. If there's a switch in the play, Player A, the screener, should roll to the basket, take a big drop step, and have her "belly to the ball," meaning she is now facing the ball. As the defense goes to the player with the ball, Player A is wide open on the roll.

Limit the Dribbles during One-on-One Drills

When you have your players play one-on-one, it's a good idea to limit the dribbles they take while completing the drill. Have them make one good fake and then drive hard to the basket. It's okay if they don't score. The point of these drills is to teach players how to play with a defender on them and to drive to the basket. This is an invaluable skill—one of the most difficult things to guard against in basketball is the drive to the basket.

Why Shoulder to Shoulder?

When you teach your players to screen for their teammates, you need to stress the importance of close contact as they come off the screen. By coming off the screen shoulder to shoulder, the teammates protect themselves from defenders coming in to block a pass or steal the ball. You can practice this without the ball at first.

Drills for the Fast Break

Fast Break O9

Divide your players into three groups, with one group right underneath the basket on the end line and the other two groups on the line on either side (see diagram at right). Player 1 under the basket starts dribbling down to the other end of the court. The first players in the other groups run wide. The dribbler stops at the foul line and makes a bounce pass to either of the other two players to complete the drill. The three players then run down the side of the floor and return to their groups. To keep the action going, send off the second set of players as soon as the first three players cross the mid-court line. Remember to emphasize *sprinting* down the floor.

Fast Break with Layup O10

This drill adds a layup to the Fast Break drill. As before, divide your players into three groups, with one group right underneath the basket on the end line and the other groups on the line on either side. Player 1 under the basket starts dribbling down to the other end of the court. The first players in the other groups run wide. The dribbler stops at the foul line and makes a bounce pass to either of the other players, who then makes a layup. The three players rebound the ball and run down the side of the floor to return to their groups. The second set of players may start out as soon as the first three players cross the midcourt line. And again, remember to emphasize *sprinting* down the floor.

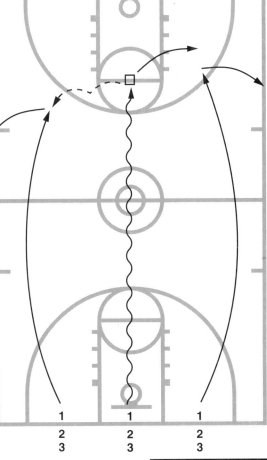

Fast Break drill

Fast Break Rebound and Outlet O11

In this drill your players learn to rebound a ball, make an outlet pass to start a fast break, and run hard down the side of the floor to receive a

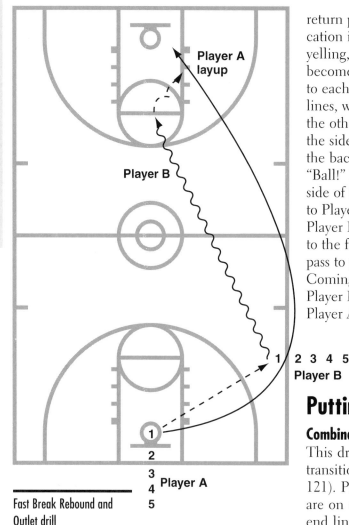

Player A
layup

Player B

1 2 3 4 5
Player B

1

2

3
4 Player A
5

Fast Break Rebound and
Outlet drill

return pass (see diagram at left). Communication is vital for a successful fast break, and by yelling, "Ball!" and "Outlet!" your players become accustomed to talking the play through to each other. Divide your players into two lines, with one line under the backboard and the other line along the foul line extended to the sideline. Begin by throwing a ball against the backboard. Player A catches it and yells, "Ball!" Player B, the first player in line on the side of the floor, yells, "Outlet!" Player A passes to Player B and runs wide down the floor, while Player B dribbles to the other end of the court to the foul line. Player B then throws a bounce pass to player A, who then goes in for a layup. Coming back the other way, the roles reverse: Player B catches the rebound and passes to Player A, who dribbles down the sideline and stops at the foul line before making the pass. ☞

Putting It All Together

Combination Transition 012

This drill works on offensive and defensive transition, fast break, and give-and-go (see page 121). Players X1 and X2 are at the elbows and are on defense. Players O1 and O2 are on the end line and are on offense. Stand between the two defenders and pass the ball to Player O2. Player X2, who's guarding Player O2, has to run all the way to touch the end line and then sprint to get back on defense. Player X1, meanwhile, goes all the way back on defense. Players O1 and O2 now start a two-player fast break down the floor, running wide. It's going to take Player X2 longer to get down the floor, so for awhile, until Player X2 gets back, Players O1 and O2 come down the court on what is known as a *two-on-one* drill. If Player X1 goes to cover Player O2, Player O2 would see Player O1 open and pass the ball to him. If Player X2 catches up, have the four players play two-on-two down that end of the floor until the defensive team gets the ball. Then the players come back up the court, with Players X1 and X2 on offense and Players O1 and O2 on defense. Again, let them play two-on-two, encouraging a drive or a give-and-go (see 06).

It doesn't really matter what happens during the course of this drill—

whether a team manages to do a give-and-go, make a basket, or turn over the ball. The point is to give your players a feel for playing two-on-two, making both offensive and defensive transitions, and playing together as a team. Later you can build this drill into a three-on-three and four-on-four. 👉

Three-Player Combination Transition 013

This is the same combination transition drill as above, but you extend it by playing three players on a side and eventually adding a fourth. Begin the drill by passing to one offensive player, whose defender has to run to touch the end line and then sprint the floor. This is a three-on-two break going down, and when it comes back it's a three-on-three. (See the Combination drill above for a full explanation of how the drill is set up.) Once players get used to this drill as a three-on-three, add a fourth player. Players then go down the court four-on-three and come back four-on-four. 👉

Adding Players to Drills: Going to Two-on-Two

Two-on-Two 014

You can add defense to the mix and work on some two-on-two drill options (see page 122). Begin with a pass and screen away. Make this a two-on-two drill by placing yourself or an assistant coach on the weak side (the side without the ball). Have Player O1 pass to the coach, who is not being guarded. Players O1 and O2 both have a defender guarding them, Players X1 and X2. The offensive players try to free each other on a screen away play or a screen away concept to receive a pass from the coach; then remove yourself or your assistant and have them play two-on-two. As soon as Player O1 or O2 makes a basket or the defenders get control of the ball, Players X1 and X2 go to the end of the offense line, and Players O1 and O2 go to the end of the defense line (see 07). 👉

Drills Using Formations

Easy Out-of-Bounds Play 015

Set up Players 2 to 5 in a box where Players 2 and 3 are at the elbows and Players 4 and 5 are on the blocks. Player 1 passes the ball inbounds.

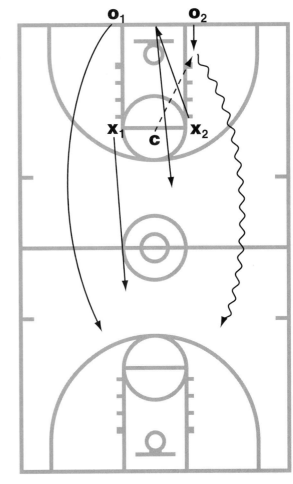

Combination Transition drill

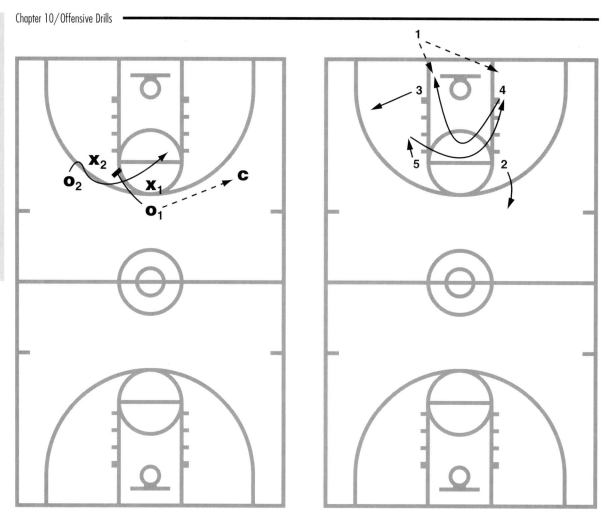

Above Left: Two-on-Two drill

Above Right: Intermediate Out-of-Bounds Play

Players 4 and 5 screen for Players 2 and 3 and then open up to the ball. Players 2 and 3 come off the screen and go to the hoop to receive the pass from Player 1.

Another variation of this play is to line up Players 4 and 5 on the ball-side elbow and block, with Players 2 and 3 on the weak-side elbow and block. Players 4 and 5 screen away Players 2 and 3. Players 2 and 3 come off the screen and go to the ball side. One of them receives the pass from Player 1 and takes a shot. 👉🏀

Intermediate Out-of-Bounds Play 016

This is a set box play designed to bring the ball from out-of-bounds down to the basket (see diagram above right). It uses a diagonal pick and roll and has a lot of deception with some good screening angles so that young players can be successful. Line up your players on the sideline, with Player 1, who will be the point guard, taking the ball out-of-bounds. Player 3 will line up on the block on the ball side, with Player 5 above Player 3 at the foul line. Player 4 is on the other side on the block, and Player 2 is at the foul line above Player 4.

When Player 1 yells, "Go!" Player 2 pops to the corner, and Player 4 comes up to set a diagonal pick and roll. Player 5, who's at the elbow, takes a step just like she's going to the corner or to the wing to receive a pass; then she cuts right off Player 4's screen to the weak-side block for a layup. As soon as Player 4 sets the screen for Player 5, she rolls down the lane right for Player 1. Meanwhile, Player 3 has popped to the corner. Either Player 4 or 5 is open every time as players learn to execute the screening action. 🏀

Down and Back 017

This is a five-on-five full-court scrimmage, where you'll have five offensive players and five defensive players. The team with the ball lines up in a three-two formation with a point, two wings, and two corners. (See page 39 for more information on formations.) Since you should be encouraging your players to move, don't worry much about formations after the initial possession. Let the kids get used to moving. The main point is that after they pass, they cut to the basket, they set a screen on the dribbler's man, or they try to free a teammate by screening and communicating the screen by saying, "Use me." It's fine if they want to drive to the basket: it keeps them aggressive, and a shot at the basket shouldn't take them long. If a basket is made, take the ball out-of-bounds and have the team previously on defense bring it down the court. If there is no basket made, then it's a transition, and the other team gets the ball. Either way, let your players play down and back, and then stop the drill after the team that originally had possession regains it. Evaluate the scrimmage with your players. Talk about what went wrong, who didn't sprint the floor, or who didn't take advantage of someone who was open. Remind them to keep their heads up or give them any other pointers for improvement. After this group has discussed their play, send them out and start another group going down and back. 🏀

Quick Reversal 018

Divide your players into three lines, with one line in the center of the court and a line on either side. The object of this drill is to move the zone with quick passes. Player 1, in the center line, passes to Player 2, who passes right back to Player 1, who quickly passes to Player 3. Player 3 catches the ball and shoots. Player 2 rebounds the ball and passes it out to the coach, and the three players go to the end of different lines. 🏀

Zone Offense 019

There are two basic concepts to a zone offense: you want to form an offensive triangle, and you want to move the ball quickly. In a zone offense, ball

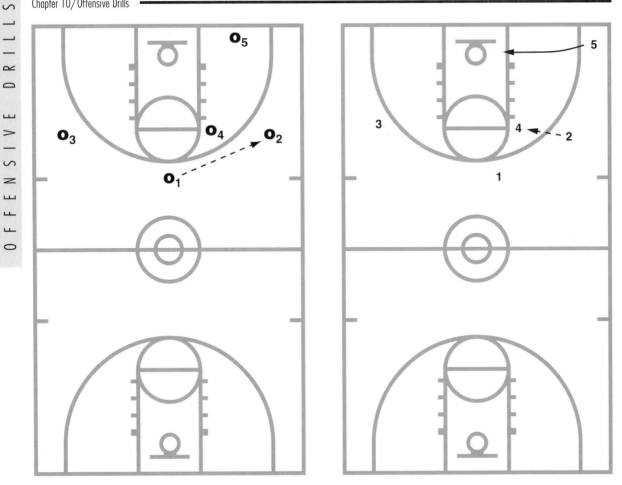

Zone Offense *(continues next page)*

movement is more critical than player movement. Against player-to-player defense, you want your players moving and cutting and driving. Against the zone, you want the ball to move (see page 40).

Player 1 is at the top of the circle. Player 2 is on the right wing foul line extended, Player 3 is on the left wing, Player 4 is at the foul line, and Player 5 is your end-line runner. This means that if Player 1 passes to Player 2, Player 5 is on the end line, in a triangle with Players 4 and 2. Player 2 either takes a shot or passes the ball to Player 4. Players 4 and 5 are partners, so Player 4 always looks for a shot or for Player 5 cutting to the basket. If the ball is passed to Player 5, he looks for Player 4 driving to the basket or for a shot.

So the ball is passed from Player 1 to Player 2. If Player 2 wishes, he can pass back to Player 1, who would swing around to Player 3 on the weakside wing. If Player 1 passes to Player 3, Players 4 and 5 come right over, creating another triangle. Player 5 is the end-line runner, so if the ball is passed from Player 2 back to Player 1, Player 5 now runs underneath the basket. If the pass goes to Player 3, Player 5 goes to the end line on that

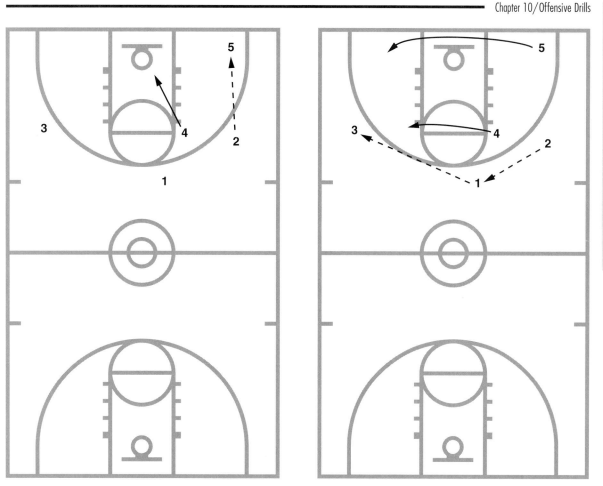

Zone Offense, *continued.*

side, creating another triangle. If the ball goes back to Player 2, Player 5 goes back to the end line on Player 2's side to form a triangle. If you form good triangles, a zone offense is hard to defend against, but players must move the ball quickly. Zones are usually beaten by ball movement and outside shots, so we're encouraging quick swing of the ball, a quick reversal of the ball right into that shot.

To work on creating a good zone offense, break down the play into a five-on-none skeleton, where the ball goes side-to-side before the players take their shots. Tell them they have to reverse the ball in this drill before somebody takes the shot. They should vary their moves so that Player 1 shoots, and Player 3 shoots, they'll hit Player 4 at the foul line, and then they'll hit Player 5, who passes it to Player 4.

Beating the Press O20

The keys to this drill are to attack the defense, dribble up quickly, and go for an easy score (see page 126). Number your players positionally from 1 to 5. Player 3 should take the ball out-of-bounds. Players 1 and 2 line up at the

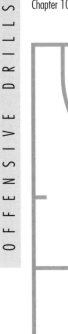

Beating the Press drill

foul line, and Players 4 and 5 line up at half-court. Players 1 and 2 try to free each other, and then Player 3 must try to get the ball to one of them. As soon as either player gets the ball, she should dribble up the floor as quickly as she can. If she can't get up the floor, there are players available to receive a pass. For example, if the ball is passed to Player 1, Players 4 and 5 are on opposite sides at half-court. Player 5 could come into the middle, and Player 4 would stay at half-court, so Player 1 would always be able to look up the ball side of the floor and to the middle. Anytime someone in the back court gets the ball, she should always look ball side to the middle. If those players are double-teamed, she could look behind the ball to the person who passed it in, which would be Player 3 (see pages 40–41). 👉

Five-on-Five Scrimmage 021

Do this drill in segments: put 2 minutes on the clock and let your players play in a gamelike situation. Call the violations and the fouls; then at the end of the 2 minutes bring the players in and talk to them about things they need to do better. Make some adjustments in regard to who's guarding whom or to make the teams be evenly matched, and then have another 2-minute scrimmage. Play five of these 2-minute scrimmages of five-on-five play. 👉

Defensive Drills

Defensive Position

Stance D1
Have your players get in the defensive stance, with a coach, assistant, or player out in front to demonstrate. Any time the coach yells, "Stance!" the whole group hits the floor with their palms, which will make sure they're low enough. Then they hold their palms out and yell, "Defense!" Try to get them to develop a defensive expression, which should be an expression of intensity and determination. When you keep them in a defensive stance for 20 or 30 seconds it is called a "burn." (Try it yourself!) Do this two or three times, making sure that they are yelling, "Defense!" and that you're giving them plenty of encouragement and positive reinforcement. ☞

Quick Hands, Quick Feet D2
From the defensive stance your players have to have quick hands and quick feet. After you yell, "Stance!" and the players respond and yell, "Defense!" you can yell, "Quick feet!" Players move their feet as quickly as possible while in the defensive stance. You can have your players do the same movements they do during the Foot Fire, where they do quarter-turns and half-turns (see Foot Fire, F4). The important fundamental here is to stay in the defensive stance and stay balanced. ☞

Tracing the Ball

Mirror F39 (D3)
Still in the defensive stance, players mirror your hand movements while you hold the ball. If you bring the ball up, their hands should trace your movement. Another variation of this drill is for you to say, "Okay, I'm a shooter and I shoot" while you motion as if you're shooting the ball. Now the kids yell, "Shot!" and put their hands up like they're contesting the shot. ☞

You can also do other defensive movements using this same command drill. If you want them to dive on the floor, for example, just say, "Okay, the ball's on the floor, everybody dive!" Players dive in their spots for a pretend ball.

Defensive Slide and Defensive Footwork

Dick Harter D4

Here's a drill named after NBA coach Dick Harter. Have your players get into a defensive position, with one foot slightly ahead of the other. Point to a direction and have the players slide their feet in quick, choppy steps. They should slide left, right, back, and forward on your signal. It's an unbelievable conditioner and difficult to do. Keep it going for 20 or 30 seconds. Do it twice. Make sure they're talking. Whenever you say, "I'm a shooter and I shoot!" they should put their hands up and yell, "Shot!" ☞

Zigzag D5

This drill helps your players work on their defensive footwork skills (see diagram at left). Line up your players in two corners of the gym and have them face the basket. Using the defensive slide, players move in a zigzag pattern from the corner to the free-throw lane to the sideline to the center circle and so on all the way up the court, making a drop step each time they change direction. When they reach the other end of the court, have them jog along the end line to the corner of the gym and start again. This drill is designed to simulate guarding a player who changes direction as she dribbles the ball. As the players do a defensive slide down the court, it is crucial to notice that their feet don't cross and that the slide isn't a hop or a skip. The slide should be quick "scoots" of the feet while the body stays low (see page 44). ☞

Figure 8 D6

This drill is another good one for working on defensive footwork. Have your players line up, run up to the midcourt line, hit the floor and yell, "Defense!" and do a defensive slide

Zigzag drill

jog   jog

defensive slide   defensive slide

1   1
2   2
3   3
4   4
5   5

across the court. They should next run backward to the end line, hit the floor and yell, "Defense!" and do another defensive slide across the court. When players get to the sideline, they should sprint down to other end of the court, ready to do the drill again.

Teaching Defense

The art of good defense is not as easy to learn as a newcomer might expect. The following drills call for players to be attentive and have some basic knowledge of the game. Though beginners can master these drills relatively easily, none of the drills are rated as "easy."

Containing the Dribbler D7

In concept, this is a simple one-on-one drill where the offensive player works on his moves and the defensive player tries to stop him. The teaching points of this drill are to emphasize to your defensive player to move his feet, keep on balance, and not foul. The defender is to stay low, keep the offensive player in front of him, and get a hand up when that player shoots. When the ball goes up to the rim, the defender should make contact with the other player and try to block him out to get the rebound.

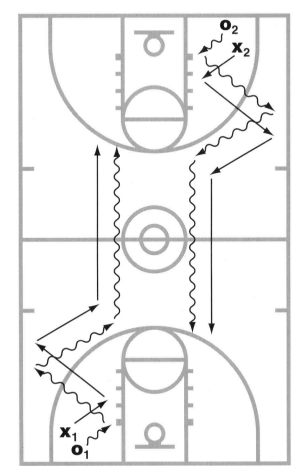

One-on-One Full-Court drill

One-on-One Full-Court D8

Divide your players into pairs of equal ability for a full-court drill, with one pair on each side at opposite ends of the court (see diagram at right). Each player with the ball has to stay on her side of the court, so you can have two pairs do the drill simultaneously. The player with the ball tries to get by the defender and make a basket at the other end of the court. The defender tries to gain control of the ball, and if the offensive player gets by her, she tries to catch up and stop the shot. The advantage for the offensive player is not having to play against two people. Play continues until the defender gets the ball or the offensive player makes a basket. Then send out a new set of partners.

Person-to-Person Full-Court D9

There will be situations in a game when your team should apply the full-court press (see page 130). (See Beating the Press O20 for the offen-

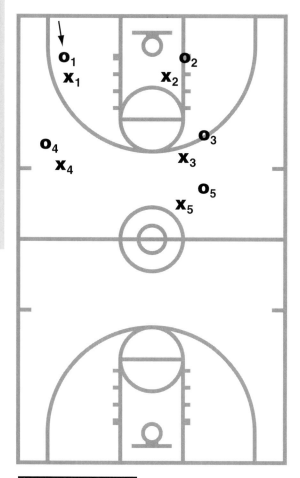

Person-to-Person Full-Court drill

sive side to this.) There are many forms of full-court pressure. I believe the best way to press at the youth level is simply to move your half-court, player-to-player game up and play it full court. Keep all the teaching fundamentals the same. Make it difficult for the opponent to get the ball inbounds. When your team scores, each player, instead of sprinting back, sprints to his man and tries not to let him receive the pass. If the ball is passed, everyone assumes the proper position. If the ball is passed to a side of the floor, the help side is established, and the formation could look like the diagram. Teach all the same concepts of help as you did in the half-court (see Defending the Basket, page 45).

Two-on-Two D10

You will have the ball in the middle of the court for this drill (see page 131). Divide your players into teams of four, with two players on offense (Players O1 and O2) and two on defense (Players X1 and X2). Place the offensive players on the wings, with the defenders guarding them. You stand center court at the key. There are several steps to this drill.

1. You pass to Player O2.

2. Player X2 yells, "Ball!" and gets in a defensive stance guarding the ball, while Player X1 leaves her man and gets in the center of the lane and yells, "Help!" It is important that Player X1 can see both the ball and her man while in the help position. An easy way to teach this is to have the help defender point to the ball with one hand and her man with the other. If the ball or her man moves, she will be able to react.

3. Player O2 passes the ball back to you in the middle, and you pass it to Player O1.

4. Player X1 moves from help-side defense to guarding the ball. She guards Player O1 by yelling, "Ball!" and gets in a defensive stance, tracing the ball. Player X2 moves to the center of the lane and yells, "Help!" pointing to the ball and her man.

5. Player O1 passes the ball back to you, and you switch your pass again to

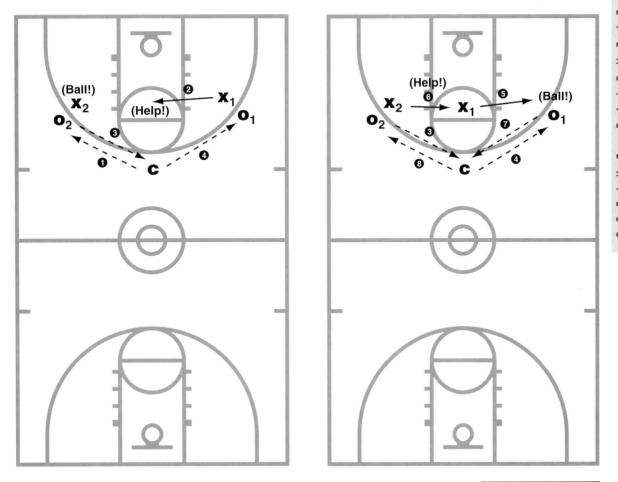

Player O2. Keep reversing the ball until your players do it well (see pages 45–49).

The Shell D11

The shell drill is designed to teach team defense. The basis of this drill is to have the defense move as the ball moves. In the beginning of the drill, the offense is stationary, and the offensive players' role is to stay in their positions and pass the ball around the perimeter. As the ball is passed around the perimeter, each defender moves with it. This drill can be done with either two-on-two, three-on-three, or four-on-four. Notice it can't be done with five-on-five because there will be a post player.

The shell drill is designed to have a clear middle, with the players around the perimeter and not clogging up the lane. Whatever formation is used, stress the concepts. If a player is guarding the ball, he yells, "I got ball" and guards his man, pressuring the ball, staying low, and being active. If a player is one pass away (meaning a close distance, either a pass from wing to corner or top to wing), then he is in a "deny" position, with a hand in the passing lane (the lane where if the ball were passed to his man he would intercept it), and in a low defensive position. If a player is more than one pass away (a skip pass from corner to corner or wing to corner), he is in the "help" position. The help position is a position having one hand pointed to his man, the other hand pointed to the ball, and one foot on the ball side with the other foot on the help side. He is in a sense "splitting the court" in two because he's directly between the two sides.

Have the offense pass the ball around the perimeter slowly at first, to make sure the kids know how to rotate from guarding the ball to deny to help and so forth. Have the defense be active but not steal the ball. The offense is stationary, so the defense will obviously hold the advantage. Once the kids have a good grasp of these concepts, try to use them. As the ball is passed around the perimeter, have the coach yell, "Go!" when an offensive player has the ball. This should start an offensive player beating his defender to the basket (with the dribble), causing the other defenders to help out. The man who is in help position should guard the offensive player and slow him down until his teammate can recover and guard him. After this process, the group can play live.

Two-on-Two Shell drill

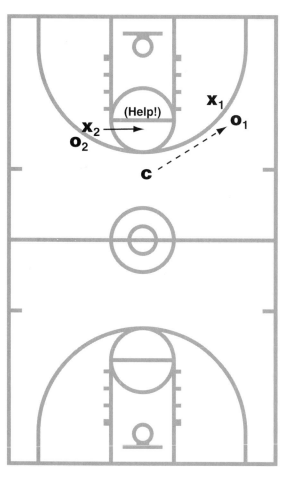

Two-on-Two Shell D12

In this variation of the shell drill, players play two-on-two at both ends of the court with a coach bringing the ball up (see diagram at left). The players work on all of the defensive principles, including ball side and help side; they learn to communicate with each other on the floor; and they are competing and having fun.

Place a coach in the middle of the floor, with Player O1 on the right wing, Player O2 on the left wing. Two defenders, Players X1 and X2 guard Players O1 and O2. The coach has the ball and starts to dribble down the center. Defenders X1 and X2 both should leave their men because the ball becomes more important than their man. If the coach passes to Player O1, Player X1 jumps out and says, "I got ball." Player X2 jumps over to the middle of the floor, points to his man, points to the ball, and says, "I got help." Then the ball is passed to the coach, and the coach passes it to Player O2. Player X2 goes from help to the ball and yells, "Ball." Player X1 says, "I got help." If the coach starts to drive between Players X1 and X2, they both would help stop the ball (see pages 45–49).

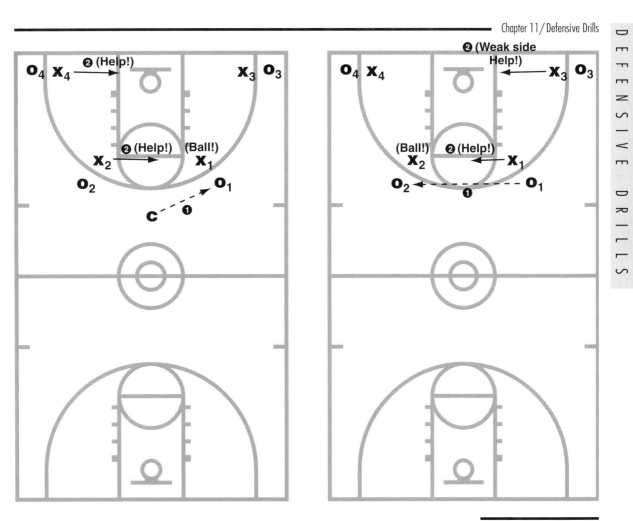

Four-on-Four Shell D13

Four-on-Four Shell drill

Divide your players into teams of four. Players O1 and O2 are at the elbows, and Players O3 and O4 are in the corners (see diagram above). If Player O1 has the ball, Player X1 is one arm's length away, tracing it in a good defensive stance. Player O2 is even with Player O1, so Player X2 is off the line of the ball toward the foul line. Player X4 is in the help position, pointing to her man and the ball, yelling, "Help!" Player X3 is trying not to let Player O3 receive the pass because Player O3 is closer to the basket than the ball. When Player O1 passes the ball to Player O2, Player X2 moves to guard the ball, yelling, "Ball!" and gets in a defensive stance. Player X1 moves to the foul line and yells, "Help!" Player X4 moves out of the help position and tries not to let her man, Player O4, get the ball. And Player X3 jumps into the lane and yells, "Weak-side help!" pointing to her man and the ball. Coach your defenders to play their particular man in relationship to the ball. Use the ball-side, help-side terminology. Rotate your players so that everyone plays each position and has a chance to do the drill (see pages 45–49).

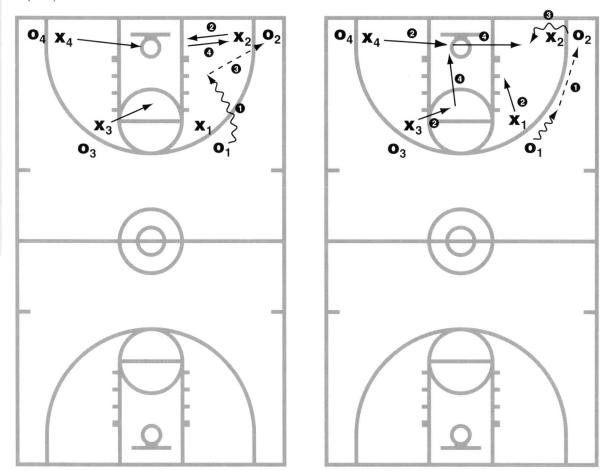

Above Left: Help and Recover drill

Above Right: Help and Rotation drill

Help and Recover D14

Help and recover is the defensive play your players will need when the ball-side defenders are forced to help stop the ball (see diagram above left). For this drill, your players are still in their shell or box set formation: Player O1 is in the right side, Player O2 is in the right corner, Player O3 is on the left side, and Player O4 is in the left corner. Player X1 is guarding O1, Player X2 is guarding O2, Player X3 is guarding O3, and Player X4 is guarding O4. Player O1 has the ball so Player X1 should be one arm's length away tracing the ball, putting pressure, yelling "Ball!" Player X2's man (O2) is closer to the basket than the ball, so X2 should try to prevent him from getting the ball. Player O3 is farther away from the basket than the ball and is being guarded by Player X3, who is off the line of the ball. He doesn't care if Player O3 gets the ball. Player X3 is also close to the line because he's one pass away—he's currently on the help side so he's going to get a foot on the ball side. Player X4 has a foot on the help side as he guards Player O4, who's in the weak-side corner. If Player O1 drives to the basket on the right side, Player X2 will leave his man and help stop the ball from getting to the basket. When Player O1 stops his dribble or passes, Player X2 will recover his man. Similarly, if Player O1 dribbles to the left, Player X3 will leave his man to help stop the ball. Once Player O1 either stops or passes back out, Player X3 will recover his man (see pages 45–49). ☞

Help and Rotation D15

Whenever weak-side help has to stop the dribbler, the whole defense rotates down to the basket (see page 134). If the ball is passed to Player O2 in the corner, Player X1 drops down because she thinks "Help!" since Player O1 is farther away from the basket. Players X3 and X4 are in the lane with one foot on the ball side. If Player O2 drives to the basket and gets by Player X2, Player X4 would go over and try to stop her. She would leave the lane and go toward the ball, driving in from that corner to stop the ball. Player X3 would drop down and help cover Player X4's man, and Player X1 would help stop the ball. All of the defenders are below the foul line in a move that is known as *help and rotation*, where players drop down to help each other stop the ball (see pages 45–49). ☞

Three-on-Three Stop Game D16

Start your players on a three-on-three offensive/defensive game where the only way they can score is by a defensive stop—the offense doesn't score. Start the game by passing with a screen away—after that players can do what they wish. Emphasize to the offensive players that if a person isn't open, they need to back-cut and be aware that the defense is trying to stop them. Play this game to four stops, and have the losers do one sprint down the court and back.
☞ → ☞

Combination Transition D17

This drill is one to incorporate into most of your practices throughout the season (see diagram at right). Your players will like it because it simulates a game situation. The skills they learn in this drill include offensive and defensive transition, fast break, and give-and-go. Players X1 and X2 are at the foul line elbows and are on defense. The coach is in the middle. Players O1 and O2 are on the end line and are on offense. Pass the ball to Player O2. Player X2, who's guarding Player O2, has to run all the way to touch the end line and then sprint to get back on defense. Player X1,

Combination Transition drill

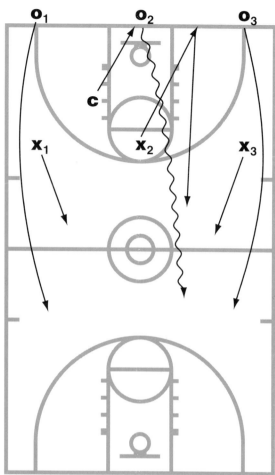

DEFENSIVE DRILLS

**Sample Three-Player
Combination Transition**

meanwhile, goes all the way back on defense. Players O1 and O2 now start a two-man fast break down the floor, running wide. It's going to take Player X2 longer to get down the floor, so until he gets back, Players O1 and O2 come down the court on what is known as a two-on-one drill. If Player X1 goes to play Player O2, this gives Player O2 the opportunity to pass the ball to Player O1, who is now open. If Player X2 catches up, have the four players play two-on-two down that end of the floor until the defensive team gets the ball. Then the players come back up the court, with Players X1 and X2 on offense and Players O1 and O2 on defense. Again, let them play two-on-two, encouraging a drive or give-and-go (see pages 37–38).

It doesn't really matter what happens during the course of this drill—if a team manages to do a give-and-go, makes a basket, or turns over the ball. The point is to give your players a feel for playing two-on-two, working on both offensive and defensive transitions, and working on playing together as a team. Later you can build this drill into a three-on-three and four-on-four (see page 41 and diagram at left).

Four-on-Four-on-Four Competition D18

Begin by having your players pass the ball around the perimeter so that they know their angles, they're calling, "Ball!" and they're calling, "Help!" Then divide your players into three teams of four players. (If you have five members on a team, one player can be a sub and can rotate in.) This is a four-on-four-on-four defensive game, where a stop (without fouling) equals a score. Don't count baskets—count stops to develop pride in the defense. The team that is on defense stays on defense until someone makes a basket.

Team A has the ball, Team B is on defense, and Team C is out-of-bounds. If Team B stops Team A, Team B stays on defense, Team A goes out, and Team C now has the ball on offense. If Team A gets a score, it moves to defense, and Team C is the offensive team. Go up to either five or seven stops to find a winner, depending on how much time you have to play. After there's a stop and you blow the whistle to change teams, you can go over what the teams are doing wrong (or right!) defensively. Make sure the teams that are making a transition on and off the court are running enthusiastically and with energy. If a team doesn't get off the court quickly, then they lose a turn. If a team doesn't come on quickly, then they go back off the court and lose their turn. Remind your teams to communicate which players they are guarding and where they are positioned on the court.

One-on-One Defensive Transition D19

With these defensive transition drills, your players learn to switch instinctively from offense to defense: they have to get down the floor first to stop the ball and play their angles to protect that basket area (see diagram below). They learn to understand the philosophy of protecting the basket, how to guard the offensive players if they are ball side, and what their responsibilities are if they are help side.

This drill underscores the importance of going on the defense as soon as the ball is in the basket. The point is to get your players instinctively turning from offense to defense. Instead of walking around and just changing lines when the ball is turned over, they get an idea that they have to sprint the floor, find their particular man, point to which player they have, call out this player's number, and then be in a position to guard.

When you are doing a one-on-one defense drill at the end of the court with Player O1 on offense and Player X1 on defense, have another player, Player O2, stand at the other end, on the foul line extended. As soon as Player X1 gets the ball or Player O1 scores, Player O1 becomes a defender and also has to guard someone (Player O2) down at the other end of the floor, so Player O1 has to turn and run the length of the floor. Player X1 passes the ball to the coach in the middle of the floor, who passes it up to Player O2, who is down at the other end of the court. Now Player O1 has to guard Player O2 after she has sprinted the whole floor (see page 41).

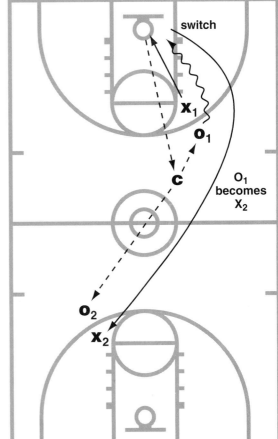

One-on-One Defensive Transition drill

Two-on-Two Defensive Transition D20

This drill is run like the One-on-One Defensive Transition drill D19 , with the addition of two more players (see page 138). Place four players at one end of the court, with two at the other end, on the foul line extended. If Players O1 and O2 are playing against Players X1 and X2, as soon as the offense scores or the defense gets the ball, Players O1 and O2 must sprint the floor and then guard the two players down at that end,

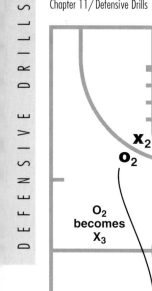

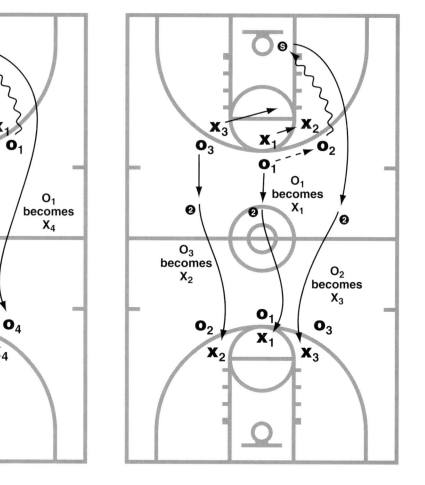

Left: Two-on-Two Defensive Transition drill

Right: Three-on-Three Defensive Transition drill

becoming Players X3 and X4. Players O3 and O4 have to sprint back and guard two new people at the other end of floor when they score (see page 41). 👉

Keep the same format of four players at one end of the court. Now put two more players down at the other end, so that Players O1 and O2 are going against Players X1 and X2, and Players O3 and O4 are at the other end. Have them play two-on-two, starting with the coach making a pass to Player O1. As soon as a basket is made, or Player X1 or X2 gets the ball, Players O1 and O2 have to sprint down the floor and guard Players O3 and O4 at the other end. Players X1 and X2 leave the floor and go back to the end of the line. Again, you get the ball in the center of the court, and Players O3 and O4 have to sprint back and guard two other people. Make them call out who they are guarding as they sprint down the floor—"I have this guy," "I have Jimmy"—make sure they are communicating. Again, start the play with a pass to Player O3. This fast-moving drill should continue until every player participates. 👉

Three-on-Three Defensive Transition **D21**

This drill is set up identically to the One-on-One and Two-on-Two Defensive Transition Drills **D19** and **D20** (see page 138). This time, however, place players three-on-three, with the remaining players waiting at the other end of the court. The team that is on offense must sprint to the other end of the court to defend as soon as a basket is made or the ball is turned over. Players O1, O2, and O3 play against Players X1, X2, and X3. Once a basket is scored or the defense gets control of the ball, Players O1, O2, and O3 must sprint down the floor to become Players X1, X2, and X3 and to pick up three other players to play against. Emphasize communication, calling "Ball!" and "Help!" and remind players to sprint down the floor (see page 41).

APPENDIX: Referee Signals

NFHS Official Basketball Signals

Glossary

Air ball: Sarcastic term to describe a shot that doesn't touch the rim.

Alley-oop pass: A pass thrown to a player who is running toward the basket. The second player leaps, catches the ball in midair, and dunks it or lays it in before he lands.

Assist: A pass that leads directly to a basket.

Back court: A team's defensive half of the court. As it refers to players, a team's guards.

Back-cut: A move in which a player takes one or more steps in a different direction than the ultimate direction in order to fake out an opponent and then goes in the intended direction in order to receive a pass or shoot. A cut to the basket, used when a player is trying to receive a pass but is being closely guarded by a defensive player who is trying to deny her the ball. Also called a *backdoor*.

Backdoor play: A fundamental basketball play in which one player passes to a teammate in the high post, and when the defenders follow the ball, another player cuts to the basket from the opposite side of the court to take a pass for an open shot.

Ball side: The side of the court (divided from one basket to the other) where the ball is. Also called "strong side."

Bank shot: A shot that is aimed at a spot on the backboard so that it caroms, or "banks," into the basket.

Baseball pass: A one-hand pass, thrown like a baseball, usually thrown far distances.

Baseline: See *end line*.

Bench: Extra players on the team available as substitutes.

Blocking foul: Illegal personal contact that impedes the progess of an opponent. When a defensive player "bodies" an offensive player who is driving to the hoop.

Blocking out: See *boxing out*.

Bounce pass: A pass that bounces on the floor before reaching a teammate.

Box set: A formation used to describe the positioning of players; in a box set.

Boxing out: The process used in rebounding, to gain position between your man and the hoop by staying low, making contact, and facing the hoop.

Brick: A hard, errant shot that caroms wildly off the basket or backboard.

Bury: Sink. To make an impressive shot, as in "bury a jumper."

Carrying: When dribbling, to place the hand underneath the ball, preventing it from returning to the floor.

Center: [position] Usually the tallest player on the court who plays in the high or low post.

Center circle: Area in the center of the court that is used for the opening tip-off.

Charging: A violation in which an offensive player runs into a stationary opponent.

Chest pass: A pass made from one person's chest to another without hitting the floor.

Crossover: A kind of dribble where the player turns his hand to the outside of the ball and pushes to the inside, so that he dribbles the ball across his body to the other hand.

Cut: A quick move by an offensive player, usually toward the basket, to get in position for a shot.

Dead-ball foul: A foul committed while the clock is stopped and the ball is not in play.

Defensive slide: When in a defensive stance the proper movement, stay low and sliding the feet, not skipping or crossing them over, more of a shuffle.

Defensive stance: The stance one uses while playing defense; staying low, knees bent, head up, hands active.

Deny the ball: Prevent an opponent from getting the ball by guarding her closely and staying between her and the player in possession of the ball.

Discovery method: A method of teaching where children discover the answer for themselves.

Double dribble: A violation in which a player dribbles the ball, stops, then begins to dribble again. Also, dribbling the ball with two hands.

Double-teaming: The defensive tactic of two players guarding one player, most commonly the player with the ball.

Dribble: Bounce the ball.

Drive to the basket: Dribbling the ball aggressively to the basket.

Drop step: A move in which the player swings one leg behind him, using his back foot like a pivot foot and opening up the legs as he changes direction.

Dunk: A shot thrown downward through the basket, with one or two hands. Also called *slam, slam-dunk, jam*.

Elbow: The corner of the foul line.

End line: The line at each end of the court, under each basket. Also called the *baseline*.

Fast break: A play in which a team gains possession and then pushes the ball downcourt quickly, hoping to get a good shot off before the other team has a chance to get back and set up on defense.

Field goal: A basket, worth either two or three points, depending on whether it was taken from inside or outside the three-point line (set at 22 feet from the basket).

Flagrant foul: Unnecessary or excessive contact committed against an opponent.

Foot fire: Moving from foot to foot as quickly as possible.

Formation: Arranging the players on the court to create space and utilize offensive skills.

Forward: [position] Either the 3, a small forward, or the 4, a power forward.

Foul: A violation. Usually, illegal contact between two players.

Foul trouble: The situation for a player is nearing the limit for personal fouls before ejection from the game, or for a team that is nearing the limit in each period after which all fouls become shooting fouls.

Free throw: An uncontested shot worth one point taken from the free-throw line after a foul has been committed against a player. Also called *foul shot*.

Front court: A team's offensive half of the court. As it refers to players, a team's center and forwards.

Full-court press: A defense used to cover the entire court. Usually played very aggressively where the defense is trying to prevent the offense from bringing the ball up court.

Give-and-go: A fundamental play in which one player passes to a teammate, then cuts to the basket to receive a return pass for an open layup or dunk.

Goaltending: A violation in which a player interferes with a shot while the ball is on its downward arc, pins it against the backboard, or touches it while it is in an imaginary cylinder above the basket; may be committed by either an offensive or defensive player.

Guard: [position] Either the 1, or point guard, or the 2, shooting guard.

Half-court line: The line at the center of the court splitting it in two halves.

Hand-checking: A violation in which a defender uses her hand to impede a player's progress.

Held ball: Or jump ball, when one or more players from each team have possession of the ball.

Help and recover: A defensive movement, used to help out a teammate by slowing down the dribbler, then recovering back to your man.

Help and rotation: A defensive movement, used to help out a teammate by slowing down the dribbler, then rotating to defend the open man.

Help side: The side of the court (divided from one basket to the other) that does not have the ball. Also called "weak side."

High post: The area around the free-throw circle.

Hook shot: A shot taken with a sweeping, hooking motion while the shooter is either stationary or running.

Hoop: Basket or rim. Also slang for playing basketball.

Inbounding: The process in which the ball is "thrown in" to start play.

Inside-out dribble: A fake crossover in which the dribbler pushes the ball "in" as if she is crossing over, then pushes it "out" to go past her man.

Intentional foul: A foul committed intentionally, not going for the ball.

Jump ball: A method of putting the ball in play in which the referee tosses the ball into the air between two players on opposing teams, who attempt to tap it to a teammate. In youth basketball, the jump ball is only used to start the game.

Jump shot: A shot taken after a player jumps in the air.

Jump switch: The process in which two defenders switch who they're guarding, most of the time during on the ball screens.

Knee to knee: The process used to swing the ball from one side to the other. It should be low, as in going from one knee to the other.

Lane: The painted area between the end line and the free-throw line near each basket, outside of which players line up for free throws. Also known as the *paint* and the *key*, because in earlier years it was key-shaped.

Layup: A basketball shot where the player lays the ball up in the corner of the square on the backboard so the ball hits the square and goes through the basket.

Loose-ball foul: A foul committed while neither team has possession of the ball, as while going for a rebound.

Low post: The area at the base of the foul lane to either side of the basket.

Man: Assigned opponent that a player is to guard.

Midcourt line: Half court line.

Mirror: Used on defense, to follow or trace the ball.

Net: The knotted cord, 15 to 18 inches long, that hangs around the basket rim's circumference.

Offense foul: A foul committed by the offensive team, that is, charging an illegal pick.

One-two stop: A legal way to stop when either dribbling or receiving the ball by having one foot land on the floor then the other.

Outlet pass: A pass thrown by a player who gets a rebound to a teammate, generally near midcourt, to start a fast break.

Overhead pass: A two-handed pass thrown over one's head.

Overtime: A five-minute extra period that is played when the game is tied after four quarters. If a game remains tied following an overtime period, additional overtime periods are played until there is a winner.

Palming: A violation in which a player moves his hand under the ball and scoops it while dribbling. Also called *carrying*.

Pass and screen away: An offensive technique used to create movement and free teammates, where one starts with the ball, passes to a teammate, and then sets a screen for another teammate, "away" from the ball.

Pass fake: A pass not made, to fake out a defender.

Penalty situation: When a team has committed more than its allotted four fouls per quarter, and thus each subsequent foul becomes a shooting foul. Also called *over the limit*.

Personal foul: see *foul*.

Pick: A play in which an offensive player jumps in the path of a defender to free a teammate for a shot by establishing a stationary position that prevents a defensive player from guarding the shooter. If the player who is "setting a pick" is not stationary and makes contact with a defender, it is an offensive foul. Also called a *screen*.

Pick and roll: A play in which an offensive player sets a pick, then "rolls" toward the basket and takes a pass from a teammate for an open shot.

Pivot: The area near the basket, generally where the center operates. Also, the act of changing directions, by keeping one foot planted on the ground while stepping in one or more directions with the other foot.

Player-control foul: An offensive foul that is committed not when a player is shooting but just when her team is in control of the ball.

Player-to-player offense: Players play man-to-man, moving, cutting, and driving.

Point guard: Usually a team's primary ballhandler and the player who sets up the team's offense.

Post: See *high post* and *low post*.

Power forward: The larger of a team's two forwards, whose duties generally involve rebounding as much as scoring.

Press: Guard very closely.

Pump fake: A fake in which a player motions as if he is going to shoot the ball but holds back, hoping his defender will jump out of position.

Push pass: A pass for younger players, where one hand guides the ball and the other drives it through to the target.

Rebound: Gather in and gain control of a missed shot; a missed shot that is retrieved.

Rejection: A blocked shot.

Reserves: See *bench*.

Runaround: An offensive tactic, where a teammate runs around the player with the ball and then cuts to the basket to receive a pass.

Sag: A defensive tactic in which a player drops off her man to help double-team a player in the pivot.

Screen: See *pick*.

Screen away: An offensive move, usually used after a player passes the ball to a teammate, in which the player moves away from the ball in order to free up the teammate by setting a screen.

Screen to the ball: An offensive in which a player moves to the person with the ball and tries to block her defender by setting a screen, thus enabling the player with the ball to dribble free of her defender.

Set shot: A shot taken while a player has both feet on the floor in a set position. This shot, common in basketball's early years, has given way to the harder-to-block jump shot.

Shell: A term used to identify the basis of defensive formation and concepts.

Shooting guard: The other guard on the floor besides the point guard. Used to mostly "shoot."

Shot clock: The 35-second clock used to time possessions. A team must attempt a shot that hits the rim within 35 seconds or else it loses possession of the ball.

Shot fake: A shot not taken, used to fake a defender into thinking that one would shoot.

Sideline: The line at each side of the court.

Sixth man: A team's primary reserve, the first substitute to enter a game.

Soft hands: A term used to catch the basketball. As opposed to "hard hand" when the ball would just bounce off. One wants soft hands to be able to catch the ball.

Square to the basket: Shoulders and feet facing the basket.

Steal: To take the ball away from the opposing team, either off the dribble or by picking off a pass.

Stop-and-go: An offensive move made of the dribble, going from full speed, then stopping, then going full speed again. Used to disrupt the defenders' rhythm.

Strong side: The side the ball is on (also called *ball side*).

Switch: When teammates exchange defensive assignments during play.

Technical foul: A violation of conduct, such as abusive language or fighting, that involves no contact with an opponent or contact while the ball is dead, and that results in a free throw for the opposing team.

Three-point shot: A field goal worth three points, taken from beyond the three-point arc.

Three-second violation: A violation in which an offensive player remains in the lane for more than three seconds.

Three sixty: A complete spin made to elude a defender, a 360-degree turn.

Tip-in: A missed shot that is tipped into the basket.

Trailer: An offensive player who trails on a fast break but often is in good position to score after the first wave of defenders goes by.

Transition: The movement from offense to defense, or vice versa, when the ball changes hands.

Traveling: A violation in which a player takes too many steps without dribbling the ball. Also called *walking*.

Triple-threat position: An offensive position where one can either shoot, pass, or dribble.

Turnover: Loss of possession of the ball, either through an errant pass or dribble or an offensive foul.

Two-footed stop: A legal way to stop when either dribbling or receiving the ball by using both feet hitting the floor at the same time.

Weak side: The side of the court away from the ball (also called *help side*).

Wing: A position on the court, by the perimeter away from the top of the three-point arc.

Zone defense: A defensive tactic in which players guard areas or zones of the court, rather than specific players.

Resources

Associations and Organizations

Alliance of Youth Sports Organizations
P.O. Box 351
South Plainfield NJ 07080
E-mail: info@aoyso.com
http://www.aoyso.com/
AYSO is comprised of local youth sports associations whose goal is to provide high-quality and safe sports programs for young people.

National Clearinghouse for Youth Sports Information (NCYSI)
800-688-5437 (KIDS)
http://nays.org/ncysi.html
NCYSI offers both an online and print catalog of books, instructional videos, and other resources related to youth sports.

National Wheelchair Basketball Association (Youth Division)
Robert J. Szyman
Commissioner
5142 Ville Maria Lane
Hazelwood, MO 63042
Phone/Fax 314-344-1982
E-mail: Youth@nwba.org
http://www.nwba.org/
NWBA is the largest and oldest wheelchair sports organization in the world. Its youth division is currently in its seventh tournament year.

National Youth Sports Coaches Association (NYSCA)
800-729-2057
E-mail: nysca@nays.org
http://www.nays.org/nysca.html
NYSCA trains volunteer coaches in all aspects of working with children and athletics. In addition to training, coaches receive continuing education and insurance coverage and subscribe to a coaching code of ethics.

National Youth Sports Officials Association (NYSOA)
800-729-2057
E-mail: officials@nays.org
http://www.nays.org/nysoa.html
NYSOA trains volunteer youth sports officials, providing them with information on the skills required, fundamentals of coaching, as well as common problems they may encounter.

National Youth Sports Safety Foundation (NYSSF)
http://www.nyssf.org/
NYSSF is a nonprofit, educational organization whose goal is to reduce the risks of sports injury to young people.

North American Youth Sports Institute
http://www.naysi.com/
NAYSI's website features information and resources to help teachers, coaches, and other youth leaders, including parents, interact more effectively with children around sports. It includes a resource section that lists books on sports and coaching, as well as two interactive sections that give a browser an opportunity to submit questions on fitness, recreation, and sports. The website's newsletter, Sport Scene, focuses on youth programs.

Parents Association for Youth Sports (PAYS)

http://www.nays.org/pays.html
PAYS provides materials and information for youth sports programs to help teach parents about their roles and responsibilities in children's sports activities.

START SMART Sports Development Program

800-729-2057, 561-684-1141
Fax 561-684-2546
E-mail: startsmart@nays.org
http://www.nays.org/startsmart.html
START SMART is designed to teach parents how to best help their children develop the motor skills necessary for a successful start in sports.

Women's Basketball Coaches Association

770-279-8027
Fax 770-279-8473
http://www.wbca.org/
This website includes information on basketball camps, news releases, upcoming events, national conventions, and publications available from the association.

Youth Basketball of America (YBOA)

P.O. Box 3067
Orlando FL 32802
407-363-9262
E-mail: yboahq@msn.com
http://www.yboa.org/
YBOA helps coaches, parks and recreation departments, YMCAs, Police Athletic Leagues, and individuals develop programs for all ages of youngsters and levels of play. YBOA offers league

development, tournaments, educational clinics, and scholarship programs. Member benefits include insurance, publications, and discounts on uniforms and equipment.

Websites and Electronic Newsletters

Adapted Physical Education

http://pecentral.vt.edu/adapted/
    adaptedmenu.html
This section of PE Central (see below) offers information to help teachers of physically challenged students. The site suggests many ways to modify sports and activities to make them accessible to all students. In basketball, for example: allow traveling; use a larger or lower goal; allow wheelchair-bound students to keep the ball on their laps; use a beeper ball and a radio under the basket; use balls of different diameter, weight, color, or texture.

Basketball Coaches Corner

http://www.cybertown.net/wi/syskos/
bb/wwwboard/index.html
This electronic bulletin board offers the opportunity to seek and offer advice; publicize tournaments, leagues, and camps; and share other types of information about coaching basketball.

Basketball Highway

http://www.bbhighway.com/
The Basketball Highway website provides a forum and resources for coaches, including news and events, coaching tips, chatrooms, and links to many other related sites.

Coaching Youth Sports

http://www.chre.vt.edu/~/cys/
Virginia Tech's Health and Physical Education program sponsors this website, which provides coaches, athletes, and parents with general, rather than sport-specific, information about skills for youth. The site also allows browsers to submit questions.

Officiating.com

E-mail: Feedback@Officiating.com
http://www.officiating.com/
This website offers news, including updates on rule changes; coaching philosophy and mechanics; and discussion boards.

PE Central

E-mail: pec@vt.edu
http://pe.central.vt.edu/
This website for physical education teachers, students, and parents is designed to provide the most current information on appropriate physical education programs, helping young people on their way to a lifetime of physical fitness and health.

Sports Parents

http://www.sportsparents.com/
Sports Parents provides a variety of articles from the magazine *Sports Parents*, a supplement to *Sports Illustrated for Kids*. Topics include coaching, sportsmanship, nutrition and fitness, equipment, sports medicine and safety, and finance and travel. A parents' tips section covers issues such as winning and losing, sibling rivalry, helping a child cope with frustration, and self-esteem.

World of Sports: Youth Sports on the World Wide Web

http://www.worldofsports.com/
This website offers a coaches forum and an extensive list of links by subject matter to other relevant sites.

Youth Sports Network

http://www.ysn.com/
Youth Sports Network is a multifaceted site with a featured sport of the week, news stories about youth sports, and a directory of sports camps. An instructional page covering basketball, soccer, baseball, and softball offers tips and ideas for both players and coaches. The site also offers information on exercise, nutrition, and first aid.

Index

Acknowledgments

This book has a little something for anyone who has ever played, coached, or watched basketball. The people most responsible for the end result are all my players, past and present, from my first junior high team with Jerry, Duncan, and Steve, to my present Dartmouth squad. These teams have provided me with an unbelievably enjoyable ride along the path of teaching and coaching, and I thank them for it. Why do a book now, after all these years? Because of Alex Kahan, president of Nomad Communications. He paved the way with his motivation, organization, and unbelievable staff. Special thanks go to Lauri Berkenkamp and Susan Hale for their knowledge, professionalism, and patience. Finally, thanks to my co-coach of 23 years, Muffy, and three special MVPs—Mike, Joe, and Scott.

About the Author

David Faucher has honed his learning-by-doing, positive approach to coaching basketball over a career spanning twenty-five years. Since 1991 he has been Head Coach of the NCAA Division I Dartmouth College Men's Varsity Basketball Team. Before then, Dave was the Assistant Men's Basketball Coach at Dartmouth from 1984 to 1991; he has coached Division II collegiate basketball and high school basketball, as well. Dave is the Camp Director of the Dave Faucher Basketball Camp, a nationally acclaimed summer youth basketball camp, which he founded in 1984. The author lives in Lebanon, New Hampshire, with his wife and three sons, all basketball players.